THE AFRICAN DREAM

Martin R. Delany

THE AFRICAN DREAM

Martin R. Delany and the Emergence of Pan-African Thought

Cyril E. Griffith

The Pennsylvania State University Press

University Park and London

Frontispiece: From I. Garland Penn, *The Afro-American Press and its Editors* (Springfield, Mass.: Willey & Co., 1891) p. 85.

This volume was published with the cooperation and support of the Pennsylvania Historical and Museum Commission in its continuing attempt to preserve the history of the people of the Commonwealth.

Copyright © 1975 The Pennsylvania State University
All rights reserved
Printed in the United States of America

Library of Congress Cataloging in Publication Data

Griffith, Cyril E.
  The African dream: Martin R. Delany and the emergence of pan-African thought.

  Bibliography: p. 140.
  Includes index.
  1. Delany, Martin Robison, 1812–1885. 2. Negroes—Colonization—Africa. I. Title.
E185.97.D4G74   973.7′092′4 [B]   74-20559
ISBN 0-271-01181-5

TO ELVINA, ORITA, AND VIVIEN

Contents

	Preface	ix
	Biographical Outline	xi
1	Introduction	1
2	Emergent Black Nationalist	5
3	Black Emigrationist Advocate	15
4	From Emigrationist to Pan-Africanist	30
5	The Journey to Africa	40
6	The African Dream Deferred	58
7	Nationalism Revisited	82
8	Pan-Africanism Reconsidered	102
	Epilogue	119
	Appendix A	122
	Appendix B	127
	Notes	129
	Selected Bibliography	140
	Index	147

Preface

Martin R. Delany was the foremost Afro-American exponent of pan-Africanism in the nineteenth century. At first he was a staunch abolitionist, but later he advocated emigration to Africa as an alternative to the black man's plight in America. This latter course made him a controversial leader among his people. Two biographies of Delany have been written in the last five years (*Martin R. Delany, The Beginning of Black Nationalism*, by Victor Ullman and *The Making of an Afro-American: Martin R. Delany, 1812–1885*, by Dorothy Sterling), but both authors concentrated more on his activities in North America than his interests in Africa. My study fills the gap on Africa and contributes to the growing body of knowledge about Delany.

I first heard of Delany eight years ago in a course on "Explorers in Africa" at Michigan State University, taught by Professor James R. Hooker. A black explorer in Africa was a unique event worthy of investigation, hence it became the focus of my dissertation. As inquiries were made about primary sources, it was evident that no single collection of Delany's papers existed anywhere. I had to search various sources in Canada, the United States, West Africa, and Britain to complete the study; and this book is the result of that adventure. It is not a comprehensive biography of Delany, but an evaluation of his thoughts on Africa and his emigration scheme. Because of this limitation, I have placed a biographical outline at the front of the book.

Many persons persuaded me to complete this study. First, Professor Hooker offered encouragement and direction while I was a graduate student at Michigan State University; his friendship during those difficult years will be remembered always. Then at the University of Ibadan Professors Jacob F. A. Ajayi, E. A. Ayandele, and Asa Davis shared their views on Delany with me, recommended appropriate sources in the university's Africana Collection, and acted as gracious hosts. Victor Ullman was a source of inspiration, too. During visits to his home we discussed various aspects of Delany's life, and he allowed me to look at materials he had collected. Lastly, I must thank Professors Hollis R. Lynch and Benjamin Quarles for their counsel. After reading the entire manuscript, they made valuable comments and suggestions. I deeply appreciate the interest these scholars have taken in my work, although all shortcomings in the book are mine.

While academicians provided inspiration for this study of Delany, librarians facilitated the search for data. In Canada, Mrs. Ethel Dewar of the Chatham Public Library was helpful. I am also indebted to librarians at the Schomburg Collection of the New York Public Library, the Moorland Collection of Howard University, the Manuscript Division of the Library of Congress, and the National Archives, and to Richard Wolf of the Harvard Medical School Library. In London I received valuable assistance from Mrs. M. B. Hughes, archivist at the Royal Geographical Society, Rosemary Keen, archivist for the Church Missionary Society, and personnel at the Public Record Office, British Museum, and the Institute of Historical Research at the University of London.

Finally, I would like to express my gratitude to those who helped financially. Funds were provided initially by the African Studies Center and the History Department at Michigan State University. Additional grants for research and the typing of the manuscript were obtained from the Liberal Arts Central Fund for Research at The Pennsylvania State University.

Biographical Outline

6 May 1812	Born in Charleston, Virginia (West Virginia)
1822	Delany family migrated to Chambersburg, Pennsylvania
1831	Martin moved to Pittsburgh
1831–1836	Attended Rev. Louis Woodson's school for black youth
1836	Began to study medicine with Dr. Andrew N. McDowell
1839	Practiced medicine (cupping, leaching, and bleeding) in Pittsburgh
15 March 1843	Married Cathrine A. Richards
1843–1847	Published and edited the *Mystery*
1848	Studied medicine with Dr. Joseph P. Gazzam
1847–1849	Co-edited the *North Star* with Frederick Douglass
1850–1851	Attended Harvard Medical School
September 1851	Attended emigration convention in Toronto, Ontario
1854	Organized Emigration Convention in Cleveland, Ohio
1856	Moved his family to Chatham, Ontario, and practiced medicine there
	Called second Emigration Convention for Cleveland
1857	Became active in local politics in Chatham
1858	Attended John Brown's convention in Chatham
	Organized third Emigration Convention in Chatham
	Appointed chief commissioner of the Niger Valley Exploring Party
24 May 1859	Left New York for journey to West Africa

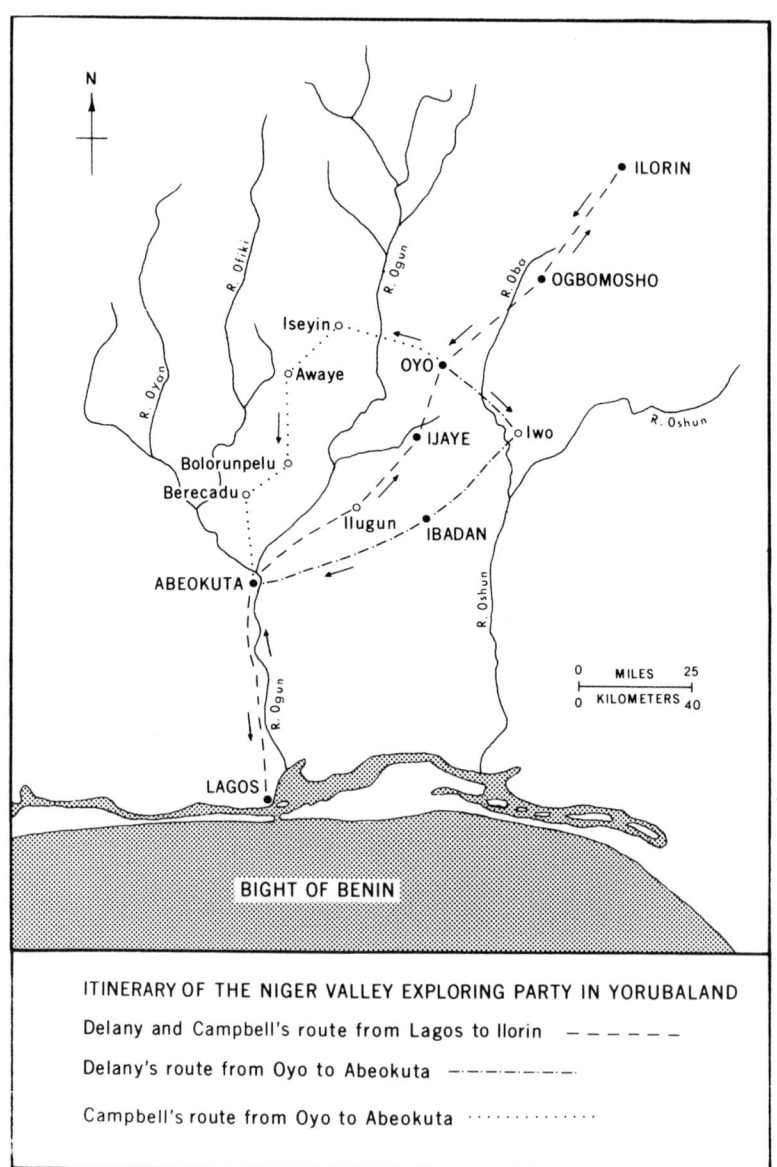

July–August 1859	Visited Liberia
20 September 1859	Reached Lagos, Nigeria
30 October–5 November 1859	From Lagos to Abeokuta
27 December 1859	Made a treaty with the Alake and chiefs of Abeokuta
January–April 1860	Delany and Robert Campbell visited towns north of Abeokuta
10 April 1860	Delany and Campbell left Yorubaland for England
12 May 1860	Delany and Campbell arrived in England
17 May 1860	Delany began lecture tour on explorations in Yorubaland
16–21 July 1860	Attended the International Statistical Congress in London
24 September 1860	Attended Glasgow convention of the National Association for Promoting Social Science
29 December 1860	Returned to Chatham, Ontario
1861–1862	Lectured in northeastern states to get support for Yorubaland scheme
1863	Became a recruiter for black regiments of Massachusetts, Rhode Island, and Connecticut
1864	Moved family from Chatham to Wilberforce, Ohio
8 February 1865	Had conversation with President Abraham Lincoln
27 February 1865	Commissioned a Major in the Union Army
15 July 1865	Assigned to work with the Freedmen's Bureau
18 September 1868	Leaves the Army
1869	Made unsuccessful attempt to become United States Minister to Liberia
1870	Nominated for national Senate from South Carolina but lost
	Opened real estate office in Charleston, South Carolina
March 1871	Ran for jury commissioner in Charleston County but lost
1872	Tried to be elected lieutenant governor of South Carolina but lost

1874	Lost second bid to be lieutenant governor
1875	Became editor of the *Charleston Independent*
	Appointed Trial Justice in Charleston
1878–1879	Joined the Liberia exodus movement in Charleston
1882	Made second effort to be Minister to Liberia but failed
	Returned to practice of medicine
1884	Returned to his family at Wilberforce, Ohio
24 January 1885	Died at Wilberforce

1

Introduction

The nineteenth century was a crucial period for black men, because of the disquieting forces of slavery and imperialism at work in America and Africa. During the century, black leaders emerged in both Africa and America to challenge white power to prevent the complete subjugation of their race. One of these leaders was Martin Robison Delany. Although born in the United States, Delany was passionately proud of his African ancestry. His attachment to the motherland became a major factor in the development of his pan-African ideology. Delany clung to the concept that black men from the New World should join with Africans to build viable nationalities on the continent. Thus he became one of the most articulate Afro-American precursors of pan-Africanism in the nineteenth century.

Throughout his long life Delany worked at various occupations. In Pittsburgh he published a newspaper and subsequently studied medicine. At the same time, he developed into an avid nationalist and eventually led a movement for emigration to Africa. During the Civil War he became the first Afro-American major in the Union Army, and remained in Charleston, South Carolina, after the war in pursuit of a political career. In the last two decades of his life Delany peripatetically returned to the practice of medicine. Delany's checkered career was understandable because the only consistency in his life was his obsession with Africa. From his mid-thirties, Delany's greatest ambition was to live in Africa permanently. As he grew older, he refused to compromise his principles of black nationalism and pan-Africanism; this steadfastness of purpose alienated many who might have helped him return to Africa. Most of all, he lost the support of his own people, for he frequently chided them for their lack of interest in and their nonappreciation of the African heritage. Yet they admired Delany's determination to pursue his goals.

Delany was one of the most unpredictable and enigmatic black leaders of the nineteenth century. It was clear that he was a black abolitionist in the 1840s. From the 1850s on, however, contemporaries and recent scholars have found it difficult to assign him a particular identity. During the later period, Frederick Douglass and other moderate black leaders labeled him as a colonizationist because he espoused emigrationism. These men were so emotionally unsettled by the emergence of the American Colonization Society that they placed black men who advocated emigration in the same category. In this study, however, a distinction is made between emigrationists and colonizationists. A colonizationist was usually a white man who thought of establishing black enclaves in Africa or elsewhere. An emigrationist, usually black, advocated migration to Africa or a Caribbean country where Afro-Americans would become an integral part of the social order in the new homeland. They disavowed the establishment of culturally exclusivistic entities in countries where the population was predominantly black. Delany and Rev. James T. Holly were men of this persuasion.

Recent scholars have begun to recognize Delany's contributions to pan-Africanism. Such Africanist historians as Hollis R. Lynch, George Shepperson, and A. H. M. Kirk-Green have alluded to Delany's work, but noted the lack of available research data. No definitive study had been made of Delany's back-to-Africa movement, its results, or its significance for the interaction of Africans and Afro-Americans in the nineteenth century. Hence this study is designed to show the role Delany played in the history of pan-Africanism. When the Civil Rights movement in the United States entered a more nationalistic phase in the late 1960s, Afro-American writers began to investigate their history and rediscovered Delany. One of these intellectuals, Harold Cruse, contended that Delany "anticipated" the tenets of twentieth-century pan-African movements in the nineteenth century.[1]

In the first decade of his life, Delany had two distinct kinds of experience that helped to determine the future course he would take. In the first instance, he gained a personal knowledge of white hostility toward blacks. On 6 May 1812, he was born of a free mother and a slave father in Charlestown, Virginia (now West Virginia). Before he was ten, however, his own father was imprisoned because he tried to prevent a white man from beating him. On the positive side, however, his maternal grandmother made him aware of his African heritage by telling him about his ancestral origins in West Africa and how his grandfather resisted enslavement in America. Through these stories, Delany learned that his grandfather was a prince whose name was Shango. Although there is no extant knowledge of the actual story Delany's grandmother conveyed to him about his grandfather's name,

Shango, there is little doubt that she gave him the impression that the deity of the same name symbolized supernatural power to the Yoruba people.[2] This might have caused Delany to think in terms of the potential power of black people. Thus the harsh reality of the adverse circumstances of black men in America and the ideal of a personal link with Africa were imprinted indelibly on Delany's young mind. As he grew, both experiences became motivating forces in his thrust for a black nationality.

As a child, Delany also learned that free blacks were victimized by Virginia laws that restricted their social mobility and the opportunity to educate their children properly. A new law passed in 1819 prohibited black children from attending schools or receiving any instruction.[3] Delany did obtain some rudimentary learning, however, when a sympathetic white peddler gave his family a primer and speller from which the Delany children learned to read and write. In 1822, when the local authorities heard that the Delany children could read, Delany's mother was summoned to court in Charlestown and found guilty of violating the 1819 law. To avoid punishment, she fled to Chambersburg, Pennsylvania, with Delany and his four older brothers and sisters. Delany's father joined his family in 1823, after he had purchased his freedom from his master in Martinsburg, fifteen miles from Charlestown. Until he was eleven, then, Delany had experienced the disjointed family life that resulted from the odious black codes of Virginia. Although allowed to marry legally, his father had not been allowed to stay with the family in Charlestown; the Delanys were not a complete family until 1823.

Delany began his formal education in Chambersburg, but there is little knowledge about him until he was nineteen years of age, when he left his family to continue his education in Pittsburgh. There he studied under Rev. Louis Woodson, who was employed by Afro-Americans in the city to teach their children because they were not allowed to attend the public schools. Five years later, Delany left Woodson's school to begin the study of medicine with Dr. Andrew N. McDowell. Perhaps it was in Pittsburgh that Delany first experienced the inner conflict which later kept him from remaining at a single occupation for a long period of time. While he yearned for a proper education in medicine, the impulse to engage in causes to help his people was even stronger. During the decade of the 1830s, the latter tendency was nurtured by his activities and experiences in Pittsburgh.

Delany arrived in Pittsburgh in 1831, the year of the dramatic Nat Turner insurrection at Southampton, Virginia. According to his early biographer, once Delany considered the incident and its consequences, he swore that henceforth he would work for the redemption of his race. Delany thereupon joined various organizations that attempted to improve the lot of his people. At first he became a member of such benevolent organizations as the Abstinence Society and the Philanthropic Society. He was the executive secretary of the latter, which helped many fugitive slaves to freedom in the North. Later, Delany belonged to a brigade of black vigilantes, who resisted white efforts to destroy Pittsburgh's Afro-American community. In 1839, after witnessing the violence whites generally employed to suppress blacks in a northern city, Delany visited the southern states of Louisiana, Texas, and Arkansas, where he saw also the viciousness of slavery. This experience led Delany, after twenty years, to write a novel on slavery, *Blake or the Huts of America*.[4]

Delany's early experience of white racism, then, became the chief motivation for his nationalism. In his formative years he had seen the degradation of slavery in the South, and he had witnessed prejudice against free blacks in the North. After observing such outrages, Delany decided to be a spokesman for his people's rights. As he grew older, however, he embraced emigrationism. Although his effort to take some of his countrymen to Africa was unsuccessful, Delany emerged as one of the earliest exponents of pan-Africanism.

2

Emergent Black Nationalist

By the 1840s, free blacks in the North were thoroughly aware of white hostility toward them. They were denied suffrage in many states because it was commonly held that they had no civil rights.[1] Furthermore, white Northerners frequently went to great lengths to keep black men from improving themselves economically. They feared job competition and often rioted when blacks were given positions which hitherto had been held by whites.[2] Despite white hostility, northern blacks strove to develop a meaningful life for themselves. Hence, by the 1840s Afro-Americans had organized their own fraternal associations, schools, and churches and published their own newspapers in northern urban communities which had sizable black populations. Through the Afro-American press, black abolitionists were able to express their views freely on the issue of slavery and the general upward mobility of their race in America. During the decade, Delany joined the growing band of black journalists when, in Pittsburgh, he began publication of the *Mystery* in 1843.[3] At first he was the sole proprietor, but he found it difficult to carry the financial burden alone. For this reason, a six-man committee assumed the business responsibilities for the paper, and Delany remained its editor until 1847, when he became a journalistic partner of Frederick Douglass.[4]

The same year that Delany began the *Mystery* he married Cathrine A. Richards, who had an Irish mother and an Afro-American father.[5] From this union came thirteen children, four of whom died as infants. Significantly, Delany named his children after famous black men; among them were Toussaint L'Ouverture, Alexander Dumas, Faustin Soulouque, Rameses Placido, and Charles Lenox Remond. These names indicated Delany's deep pride in the achievements of black men in various parts of the world. Moreover, they represented the black man's potential in a world which generally thought of him as a person of limited talents.

Delany frequently used the *Mystery* to express his nationalist ideas. A contemporary editor commented that "One would almost think that he was back in old Africa, surrounded by the noble fathers."[5] Even when Delany's journalism was less strident, he excited readers when he wrote about local issues. He often spoke out against discrimination in the North, especially when he was its victim. On one occasion in Columbus, Ohio, he had not been allowed to ride in a stagecoach after he had purchased a ticket, and some time later he received the same kind of treatment in Buffalo, New York. In an explanation of the historical significance of the *Mystery*, Delany concluded that it was the only newspaper "in the West (Pennsylvania, Ohio, and Michigan) which faithfully defended the rights of our people."[6] At times his candor prompted charges of slander.

Delany once attracted a considerable amount of public attention when he castigated a black man, Tom "Fiddler" Johnson, for assisting white men who captured fugitive slaves in Pennsylvania. He was sued for libel, and the trial was held in the Court of Common Sessions of Allegheny County in late March and early April 1847. The court found Delany guilty and fined him $150, with court costs of $25. However, many people felt that the fine was excessive. In the ten days allowed Delany to collect the money, his lawyer, William E. Austin, local newspapers, and antislavery sympathizers launched a campaign to gain public support against the court's decision and petitioned Governor Francis R. Shunk to intervene in the case. No doubt because the fine had been the highest assessed in a libel case in Pittsburgh, the governor rescinded it, but not the court costs.[7] Despite the conviction, Delany continued to speak out against the retrieval of fugitive slaves in Pennsylvania. Because of his boldness, antislavery advocates saw Delany as one of the most dedicated, articulate, and courageous black leaders in Pennsylvania:

> Dr. Delany deserves great credit for the efforts he has made for the elevation of his race in this country. Supporting himself and his family by his profession, he gives his services gratuitously as the editor of the *Mystery* . . . which he conducts with energy, intelligence and skill. He is self educated, and owes all that he is to his own resolution and perseverance. With intellectual powers considerably above mediocrity, he is possessed of energy and determination. . . . He exhibits in his person, if any such exhibition were necessary, proof of the capacity of the negro [*sic*] for eleva-

tion, there being nothing in his appearance to denote the slightest tincture of Saxondom in his blood.⁸

As editor of the *Mystery*, whether writing about slavery or politics, Delany uncompromisingly attacked individuals and institutions. But his assault on racial enemies was even more evident when he co-edited the *North Star* with Frederick Douglass from 1847 to 1849. He first met Douglass in Pittsburgh in 1846, after Douglass had returned from Europe. Delany was so impressed by the opportunity to work with the greatest black antislavery advocate of his time that he relinquished his editorship of the *Mystery* to join Douglass in the publication of the *North Star*. While Douglass published his newspaper in Rochester, New York, Delany remained in Pittsburgh as its western agent and editorial correspondent. His name was on the masthead of this newspaper from the first issue of 3 December 1847 until 1849 when Delany terminated his partnership with Douglass.⁹

By the time he was thirty-five years of age, Delany had become one of the fearless spokesmen for the fair treatment of Afro-Americans. He had proved his boldness as the editor of the *Mystery*, and in 1848 he revealed this quality again as a traveling abolitionist crusader in western Pennsylvania, Ohio, and Michigan. On the tour, however, Delany diverged from Douglass ideologically when he suggested that black abolitionists needed to seek a new direction. They had been slow to urge Afro-Americans to initiate action against slavery and to press for economic and social betterment. Instead, black leaders had relied too much on the assistance of white abolitionists. Delany's independence of mind and the forthrightness exhibited during the westward tour contributed greatly to the dissolution of the Douglass-Delany partnership.

Concerning Delany's lectures, one white man observed, "Mr. Delany is a colored man, and labors under the disadvantages of that class, yet he is represented by those who have heard him, as an entertaining speaker, and will please any reasonable man";¹⁰ Delany, however, had no intention of merely entertaining his mixed audiences or being reasonable. He intended to make them aware of the bitter realities of slavery and the prejudice against free blacks in the North. He wanted his listeners to know that despite limitations on the black minority in America, they would rise above their circumstances and take their rightful place beside other men. This was the tone of a letter he wrote to Douglass on the eve of his westward tour, in which he said, "I will never cease to cry aloud until I, and every wronged and oppressed son and daughter of America and the world, stand up in the living image and dignity of manhood, in the full possession of all those rights and privileges common to our nature, made sacred by the God of Love!"[11]

Delany believed that Afro-American entrepreneurship was a vital aspect of self-determination, and he looked for evidence of it wherever he traveled. He felt a measure of pride when he saw black-owned lumber and coal companies in York, Pennsylvania, Afro-American farmers and mechanics in Chillicothe, Ohio, and carpenters, shoemakers, painters, plasterers, and bricklayers in Columbus. Delany's concept of black entrepreneurship was based on a simple maxim which he wrote into the resolutions of a business committee presented to the Afro-American National Convention which met in Cleveland in early September 1848. He argued "that whatever is necessary for the elevation of one class is necessary for the elevation of another."[12] In other words, the economic pursuits of white people in America spurred the growth of the nation. If blacks hoped to attain greatness in the United States or elsewhere, they also must engage in a variety of economic activities.

Although he saw black men engrossed in positive economic pursuits, Delany was upset by the menial positions many Afro-Americans held in the North. These conditions motivated him to speak to black audiences about their subordinate economic position. He declared that freedom would mean little if black men held mainly unskilled jobs, and less if Afro-Americans resigned themselves to such a fate. Because of his growing nationalism, however, Delany often alienated his fellows when he discussed economic self-determination. At the Cleveland convention he declared he would prefer to see his family dead rather than employed at menial jobs, and he accused those attending of complacency. Four years later he argued that Afro-Americans hardly could have a respectable status in American society when they were only accorded subservient economic roles. Delany said, "We cannot at the same time, be domestic and lady; servant and gentleman."[13] To offset the trend toward a servile economic role, the emergent nationalist advised his people to seek an industrial education and to establish their own businesses. If successful, it would be possible in the future for Afro-Americans to engage in commercial enterprises with black men in the West Indies and Africa. In this instance, Delany went much further than Douglass and other black abolitionist leaders. He saw Afro-American economic growth as an important prerequisite to any future economic cooperation between disparate groups in the black diaspora. Advocacy of economic self-determination was one of the root causes for Delany's back-to-Africa scheme in 1859.

Another persistent theme in Delany's lectures was the absolute necessity for a political awakening among Afro-Americans. Black men needed to acquire a thorough knowledge of politics to assert their rights in America and to share power with whites. If black men developed their political awareness and expanded their knowledge of the world, white men necessarily would change their concept of them as members of an inferior race, and blacks could demand an equal share in developments at home and abroad. Thus, many years before W. E. B. DuBois, Delany foresaw the need for a political awakening among black men that was international in scope, making him one of the earliest contributors to the evolution of a pan-Africanist ideology.

Delany believed that he, Douglass, and other black leaders had a specific responsibility to politicize the black masses in America. Only they could take the initiative for their own advancement, represent their own causes, present their own claims, and address their own wrongs to the American people. They had to raise their own money to establish and maintain institutions and public figures, and not rely on white philanthropy. To accomplish all of these goals, Delany told Douglass that black leaders needed to form a "tract association" to print and distribute pamphlets that dealt with Afro-American problems and emphasize black self-determination. By 1849, then, Delany had developed nationalistic ideas, and he implored his friend and colleague, Douglass, to follow his lead. It was a time for black abolitionists to change their tactics because their goals differed from white abolitionists. The black community in the North had to learn that they had a separate destiny which went beyond mere freedom from slavery and the right to equality in America. It was a destiny that accorded black men equality with whites in political and economic affairs.

Although Delany spoke enthusiastically about the need for black men to elevate themselves, he knew there were arbitrary and continued barriers in America that would make it difficult to realize nationalist goals. He was disturbed greatly by the poor education that black youth received because of northern segregation of schools. He deplored the "black codes" of Ohio that made Afro-Americans pay taxes for a public school system that did not accept black children. Finally, he was appalled by the fact that only five black students were enrolled at Oberlin College when he visisted that institution in 1848. Because of these observations Delany declared vehemently, "let their acts of wickedness and despotism be exposed upon the house top, until they shall learn to respect the rights of man, and administer equal and evenhanded justice to all."[14]

The inadequate education of young Afro-Americans did not prepare them to be productive and competitive adults. Moreover, it made them apathetic and complacent about their responsibility to continue many of the enterprises their fathers had started and impervious to the future needs of their race. He said, "the young people, as such, especially the young men, have not in general come up to that standard of duty which the three millions of American slaves, and six hundred thousand nominally free colored people of the nonslaveholding states, so loudly call for and imperatively demand."[15] Poorly educated black youth were stumblingblocks to black self-determination.

Although there were barriers to black progress in the larger American community, Delany believed a major obstacle to self-determination existed within the black community. He felt that Afro-Americans were too preoccupied with Christianity and ignored the struggle for earthly goals. Such religiosity was one of the effects of slavery which black men had to overcome.[18] His criticism of the religious tendencies of Afro-Americans provoked protests from his contemporaries. Delany nonetheless insisted that the upward mobility of Afro-Americans was contingent upon placing faith in its proper perspective. At no time did he urge black men to give up religion but to recognize that, if wrongly used, it could make them weak rather than strong.

Because of Delany's forthright statements on slavery and his persistence in espousing black self-determination, he was not always received enthusiastically on his westward tour. His speeches were often more radical than his traveling black abolitionist associates, Charles Lenox Remond and John Mercer Langston. Many Afro-Americans in Ohio expressed concern at Delany's outspoken demand for immediate emancipation, but they were also proud to see a black leader speak with such conviction and determination.

On many occasions, white antislavery enthusiasts were not overjoyed at Delany's radical oratory. He was shocked when the Quakers of Columbiana, Ohio, refused to let him lecture in their meetinghouse. From this experience Delany altered his opinion of the Quakers. He said, "How can these misnamed 'Friends' reconcile themselves to their course in this respect? I cannot conceive that there is much Christianity where there is no humanity."[16] The Columbiana incident was not an isolated event. Delany had received similar treatment in Cincinnati, where he concluded that white proponents of antislavery were mainly interested in conservative black abolitionists, but not those making "a declaration of truth."[17]

White opposition to Delany's crusade in the West reached its highest point in Marseilles, Ohio. John Mercer Langston and he planned to hold a meeting there 28 June 1848, but a mob of white men congregated in front of their hotel and dared them to come outside. The rabble hurled epithets at the black abolitionists and threatened to burn the hotel. By morning, however, only six men were left, and they threw stones at Delany and Langston as friends helped them to escape. Thus Delany's experience in the West as an antislavery orator and agent for the *North Star* was partly a frustrating experience. There was much hostility against antislavery advocates—particularly against black abolitionists—in many of the communities he visited. General white opposition and some black indifference to his radical positions convinced Delany that Afro-American leaders needed to devise some independent means of improving their condition in America and elsewhere.

He had been moving away from the moderate views of Douglass and other black leaders with regard to the upward mobility of Afro-Americans. Douglass, particularly, favored common action for all abolitionists, but Delany favored an independent black stance. The differences in their respective positions was clearly evident in the way they perceived the purpose of the *North Star*. Douglass saw it as a terror to "evil doers" but "freely opened to the candid and decorous discussion of all measures and topics of a moral and humane character, which may serve to enlighten, improve and elevate mankind."[18] Douglass was forthright in his statements against slavery, but he was very careful not to make assertions that would alienate the support of those whites who could assist black men in their struggle for freedom and equality. Delany, on the other hand, cared little whether he offended those whom other black leaders considered friends of the race. He saw the *North Star* "as a liberal, high moral, anti-sectarian, independent, unyielding and uncompromising enemy to that most blighting of all curses, and 'abomination of abominations'—Slavery."[19] His refusal to compromise and his insistence that black men rely on their own initiative and direction severely strained his relations with Douglass by the time he completed his westward tour.

The contrast between Delany's radicalism and Douglass's moderation became obvious to the readers of the *North Star* when Douglass issued a statement in the paper which indicated he no longer was willing to assume the responsibility for the caustic comments Delany made. Douglass declared that "in compliance with the wishes of numerous correspondents, we shall hereafter append our own initials—F. D.—to all articles from our pen published in the *North Star*. Our friend and colaborer, M. R. Delany, will probably append his initials to articles written by himself. This arrangement is adopted solely to gratify our readers, and not because there is the slightest division of sentiment between ourselves."[20] If Douglass was complying with the wishes of the readers, it was apparent to them that there was an increasingly marked difference between the positions of the two leaders on matters pertaining to the Afro-American community. Because they were unable to reconcile their ideological conflict, Douglass and Delany eventually dissolved their journalistic partnership.

There were also other reasons why Delany ended his relationship with Douglass as co-editor of the *North Star*. By the fall of 1849 he had become disillusioned with black abolitionist leaders. His radical statements and his emphasis on black self-determination without white philanthropy put him on the periphery of the circle of black leaders in the abolitionist movement. The nationalist advocate avowed, "I have never been sufficiently successful in the cause of our brethren to have a value set upon my efforts. I have labored for nought, and received nothing."[21] Convinced that he had not fully impressed his abolitionist colleagues to embrace a more nationalistic stand, Delany decided to withdraw from this circle to try and actualize his concept of black self-determination. Delany also left the *North Star* so that he could devote more attention to his family. The Congressional debate in 1849 for a more effective slave law caused great anxiety in northern black communities. In addition, hostile whites often threatened the black community of Pittsburgh where he lived. Delany felt that he had given much for the antislavery cause and that it was time for him to see to the welfare of his family.

Aside from ideological differences with other black abolitionists and the impending threat of a fugitive slave law, Delany wanted to complete his studies in medicine and at age thirty-eight he tried to enter medical schools in Massachusetts. In the fall of 1850, he applied to the Berkshire Medical School at Pittsfield, Massachusetts. He had several recommendations from doctors and ministers in Pittsburgh and Allegheny City, Pennsylvania. The medical men attested to Delany's upright character and to his ability to study medicine. Dr. Joseph P. Gazzam of Pittsburgh, with whom Delany studied from October 1846 to March 1848, highly recommended him and noted that other doctors respected his medical abilities. Dr. F. Julius LeMoyne, with whom Delany worked for a year before applying to Berkshire, told the faculty they would be doing a service to "the cause of science, justice and humanity" if they allowed him to study at their institution.[22] Among the clergymen, Rev. A. W. Black of the Reformed Presbyterian Church in Pittsburgh not only referred to Delany's "high morals" but also classified him as a man with great intellectual powers; other ministers concurred with Black's estimate.[23]

Despite such overwhelming evidence, Delany's chances for admission to the Berkshire Medical School were slim. According to Professor Henry H. Childs, one of the founders of the medical school, the administration was reluctant to admit black men who did not intend to practice in Liberia and who were not sponsored by a colonization society. Between 1846 and 1850, Berkshire enrolled three black men, who were supported by the Massachusetts Colonization Society and who planned to practice in Africa.[24] Delany had no intention of going to Liberia under the auspices of any colonization society, and the Berkshire Medical School would not let him earn a degree there to practice in the United States.

Denied entry to Berkshire Medical School, Delany turned to Harvard University where the Massachusetts Colonization Society recently had placed two black men who planned to practice in Liberia, Daniel Laing, Jr., and Isaac H. Snowden. They entered the university's medical school in time for the fall term of 1850; Delany arrived at least three weeks late. After presenting the recommendations he used at Berkshire, he undoubtedly was admitted to the fall lectures with the two other black students, even though he did not have the support of a colonization society. As it turned out, he, Snowden, and Laing were not allowed to return to the Harvard Medical School for the second term because some students protested.

The medical students of Harvard were divided over the issue of admitting black men into their ranks. The number of students who protested, however, was large enough to convince the faculty that their experiment in integration should not continue for the second term of 1851. Sixty medical students met in Boston on 10 December 1850 and agreed to resolutions which implored the faculty of the Medical School not to allow Snowden, Laing, and Delany to continue their studies there. They believed that the presence of black students would demean the medical school's reputation, lower the value of its degrees, and cause a sharp drop in white enrollment. They argued, moreover, that they should not be compelled to study with a class of men with whom they would not associate beyond the halls of learning. Those students who objected to the anti-black resolutions also sent letters to the medical faculty which expressed their views on the issue. They upheld integration because Berkshire Medical School, Harvard's competitor, had done so earlier. They thought it immoral for their classmates to object to a policy dictated by considerations of humanity and public right.[25]

Because of the division among the medical students over the admission of black men, the faculty had to make a conclusive judgment in the case. After considerable deliberation, they decided to let the three black students remain for the first term because they already had been admitted, but on 26 December 1850, they voted not to let them return for the second term in 1851.[26] Most of the faculty felt that their obligations to the white majority was far greater than to any experiment in interracial learning. Consequently, the Massachusetts Colonization Society was advised not to enroll Snowden and Laing for the second term because their presence had caused conflict among the white students. By January 1851, the controversy was over momentarily when the faculty assured protesting students that Delany, Snowden, and Laing would not be at the lectures for the second term.

When Delany was denied the opportunity to complete his formal education in medicine, it added another concrete example to his expanding catalogue of injustices northern whites committed against black men. It was further evidence that black self-determination would be difficult to achieve in America. More than anything else, Delany's sense of humiliation and rejection determined the course he would take in the 1850s. He was now a confirmed nationalist, the Harvard experience precluding any return to the ranks of the moderate black abolitionists. After he left Cambridge Delany aligned himself with those black emigrationists who sought a solution to the plight of Afro-Americans beyond the boundaries of the United States. They believed Afro-Americans should go to areas of the world with a black majority and work there to build viable polities and economies without white directives. Liberia was unacceptable, however, because it came under the auspices of the American Colonization Society. Delany soon became the leading ideologue for this movement and turned it from emigrationism to pan-Africanism.

3

Black Emigrationist Advocate

In the crucial decade of the 1850s some black leaders contended that emigration was the only way Afro-Americans in the North could avoid further limitations on their freedom. Perhaps the event that led many Afro-Americans to think of leaving the country was the enactment of the Fugitive Slave Law in 1850. Because of this legislation, many black people believed slavery would be nationalized, and this fear caused emigrationist sentiment to grow among northern freedmen. If the new law was rigidly enforced, many fugitives would have been returned to the South. To avoid such a fate, many escapees fled to Canada in the decade before the Civil War; at least three thousand Afro-Americans emigrated to Western Ontario between 1851 and 1861.[1] The majority of them decided, however, to remain in the United States. At conventions held in Massachusetts, New York, Ohio, and other states, black men resolved to defend themselves if the Fugitive Slave Law was vigorously enforced.[2]

In Pittsburgh, where Delany lived, there was great concern about the Fugitive Slave Law. In June 1850 at a mass meeting of black men from Pittsburgh and Allegheny City, the resolutions committee, with Delany in the chair, concluded that Afro-Americans no longer were safe from being kidnapped and reenslaved. Moreover, Delany and others believed that many Pittsburgh whites would conspire with proslavery forces to return them to bondage. To avoid this possibility, the meeting agreed to appeal to the federal government for protection. Some Afro-Americans, however, did not wait for the government's response; two hundred of them emigrated from Pittsburgh to Canada before the Fugitive Slave Law was enacted.

The Fugitive Slave Law also contributed greatly to Delany's growing disenchantment with America. In his treatise on the condition of Afro-Americans Delany wrote "A people capable of originating and sustaining such a law as this, are not the people to whom we are willing to entrust our liberty at discretion."[3] When William Lloyd Garrison raised some objections to his book, Delany reasserted his disillusionment with America's failure to apply equality to black men. He affirmed, "I have no hopes in this country—no confidence in the American people—with a few excellent exceptions—therefore, I have written as I have done, Heathenism and Liberty, before Christianity and Slavery."[4] Thus between 1850 and 1852 Delany finally reached the conclusion that equality for black people in America was virtually unattainable. If there had been any hope that he would rejoin the ranks of the black abolitionists, his reaction to the Fugitive Slave Law prevented it. He believed the North would capitulate to the proslavery forces rather than dissolve the Union, and the whole nation would become slave territory. The only logical alternative for northern free blacks was emigration to an area where Afro-Americans could work with other black men to build viable states.

While Delany was trying to complete his medical training, emigration meetings proliferated in the North. Denied the opportunity to remain at Harvard and unable to overcome his compulsion to engage in black nationalist causes, Delany sought the companionship of Afro-American leaders who saw emigration as an alternative to remaining in America. In 1851, he joined them in Toronto, where he represented Pennsylvania blacks at a historic meeting of emigrationists. Ontario was an appropriate place for emigrationists to meet because it had been a refuge for many fugitive slaves, and emigration sentiment was stronger there than in the United States. Furthermore, two of the most articulate emigrationists of the 1850s were based in Canada. They were Henry Bibb, who edited the *Voice of the Fugitive* in Windsor, Ontario, and Mary Ann Shadd, who wrote a monograph in which she urged Afro-Americans to select Canada for permanent settlement.[5] It was in Toronto, then, that Delany plunged into a new movement which he would lead within five years, fusing emigrationism with a more thoroughgoing black nationalism.

The North American Convention of Emigrationists met at the Saint Lawrence Hall in Toronto in September 1851. The first resolution declared

> that the infamous fugitive slave enactment of the American Government—whether constitutional or unconstitutional, is an insult to God, and an outrage upon humanity, not to be endured by any people; we therefore earnestly entreat our brethren of the northern and southern states to come out from under the jurisdic-

tion of those wicked laws—from the power of a Government whose tender mercies, towards the colored people, are cruel.[6]

The statement clearly revealed growing black interest in emigrationism by 1851. It also provoked considerable debate about where black men should relocate. Delany, of course, supported emigration, but at the time he desired to remain in America to criticize the Fugitive Slave Law and the activities of the American Colonization Society. A difference of opinion over the destination of emigrants was overcome on the convention's second day, when the business committee revised the resolution to indicate that Afro-Americans would be encouraged to settle in Canada but not in Africa or the West Indies. Once the emigration resolution was approved, the convention considered the recommendation for the formation of a North American League that would unite all emigrationists in North America. Emigrationists from Vermont did not attend the Toronto meeting but two of their leaders, James T. Taylor and James T. Holly, asked J. T. Fisher of Toronto to present their blueprint for the league to the convention. After Fisher outlined the proposed organization to the convention, it was approved. The league would be headquartered in Toronto, and incorporated according to Canadian law. Its board of managers would constitute an executive committee, two-thirds of whose members would reside in Toronto permanently to direct the affairs of the emigrationists between their annual sessions. To augment its work, the league was expected to appoint commissioners who would organize auxiliaries in black communities in Canada and the United States. Taylor and Holly also insisted that the organization should have a public relations department specifically to solicit support from philanthropists and generally explain the cause of the black emigrationists. Despite this bold plan, the league never materialized.

The 1851 call for the formation of an emigrationist organization was a significant development. It indicated that a segment of black leaders in the United States and Canada was anxious to take a more active and nationalistic approach to finding a solution to the unequal status of black people in America. On the other hand, it was obvious that the emigrationists had decided to sever their ties with moderates in the Afro-American convention movement. Taylor and Holly made this disassociation emphatically clear by referring to the Toronto convention as

> The sovereign representative of the colored people of the United States and the Canadian provinces. You have the supreme right to legislate for their interest, and adopt measures for their advance-

ment irrespective of any other association, so far as wisdom and prudence shall suggest. The organization that you shall establish [the North American League] cannot be auxiliary to any other similar association, but must be sovereign in carrying out its own object.[7]

Delany's and Holly's association with the Toronto convention was a happy coincidence for black emigrationists. Both favored an independent organization that would encourage Afro-Americans to leave the United States to pursue an independent existence elsewhere. Both believed the time was right for black men to direct their own affairs; they had acquired sufficient skills to build viable self-sufficient communities in some adopted homeland. Although Holly was one of the architects of the league and helped to draft the Report on Emigration for a black convention at Amherstburg, Ontario, in 1853, Delany emerged as the emigration movement's major ideologue. Delany's boyhood curiosity about black homelands beyond America had developed into an obsession because of his fierce racial pride, his sharp resentment of the abuses his people suffered in their native country, and the rebuffs he had encountered in his personal efforts to elevate himself. Thus, because of the way he conceived of the black man's role in the world and the way he reacted to his existence in America, Delany logically came to lead the black emigration movement.

During the decade after the Toronto conference, Delany diligently argued for emigrationism and the construction of a strong economy by black men in the Caribbean. He expected Afro-Americans and West Indians to organize large-scale cotton, sugar, and rice enterprises to compete against and destroy the economy of the southern states, where these commodities were produced with slave labor. Delany also believed black men were as capable of nation-building as white men. He implored his people, therefore, to broaden their vision of the world. If white men could leave Europe to establish new nations, black men had the right to quit the United States to build viable polities and economies. He concluded that black men who did not conceive of their unlimited mobility in the world were fit only to be slaves.[8] Hence activism, economic determinism, and pan-Africanism became the main tenets of the black emigrationist movement.

By 1852 Delany no longer could contain his enthusiasm about the establishment of the emigration organization called for in Toronto. In keeping with his earlier view that Afro-American leaders needed to make the black masses aware of their fate in America, he hurriedly wrote his book, *The Condition, Elevation, Emigration, and Destiny of the Colored People of the United States*. In this work Delany admitted that he first considered emigration when he was twenty-three years old. At the time, he belonged to a black club in Pittsburgh called the Literary Institution of Young Men. During its meetings, he often tried to persuade his associates to consider emigration to California, Mexico, or South America, but they were not very receptive to his ideas. Their initial rejection foreshadowed Delany's failure in the large black community, where he propagandized unsuccessfully for seventeen years.

Delany believed emigration was psychologically important for an oppressed people. People reared in subservience were prone to develop negative attitudes about themselves and their place in society; emigration would save black men from this inferiority complex. To sustain his argument, Delany referred to contemporary European immigrants in America. The freedom they enjoyed in America caused a psychological transformation that allowed their children to aspire beyond their parents' accomplishments. Such human success was not true for Afro-Americans, he contended, because free blacks were kept in menial economic roles in the North and the South. If this trend continued indefinitely, future generations of black youth would have very low aspirations. Delany argued that emigration was the only way to prevent the growth of psychological negativism among Afro-Americans.

When Delany published his book in 1852, it was not enthusiastically received by prominent black leaders, who equated black emigrationism with colonization. He was deeply hurt when Frederick Douglass and Henry Bibb did not acknowledge the book's publication in their newspapers. However, he made it clear that neither the "silent treatment" by his friends nor the objections of whites would deter him from charting an independent course for black men to follow.[9] To those who were critical of his espousal of emigration, Delany declared that such a course of action was not new. Throughout human history oppressed people had left their homes; they loved liberty more than Afro-Americans who seemed to cling to their oppressions. Thus in 1852 he adhered tenaciously to the view that black emigrationism could contribute as much to freedom for slaves as constitutional emancipation.

While Delany disliked the lack of support from black leaders, he reserved his most caustic invective for white antislavery leaders, most of whom he considered to be pseudo liberals who retarded black leadership and initiative. He admitted there were honorable men among them, but they engaged in too much rhetoric. Afro-Americans needed action in the national context, but the abolitionists never seemed to accomplish much. Moreover, he inferred that white antislavery leaders failed truly to support black upward mobility; within their own circles they made no great effort to allow Afro-Americans equal status. He said, "We find ourselves occupying . . . a mere secondary, underling position, in all our relations to them."[10] Delany concluded that Afro-Americans committed a grave error by continuing to look to white abolitionists as leaders for the black cause.

Since he believed there was no equality in the antislavery movement, Delany opposed any black-white coalition for Afro-American progress. He contended that one of the major problems of black leaders was their tendency to rely on white directives rather than pooling their own talents to work out schemes to improve conditions for Afro-Americans. At the time Frederick Douglass was consulting with Harriet Beecher Stowe to build an industrial training school for black youth. Delany criticized both, claiming that Stowe, and white people generally, knew very little about blacks and, therefore, could devise no effective scheme to benefit Afro-Americans. He was against a school that would have white administrators and teachers because it could have the wrong psychological impact on the black students. Furthermore, he insisted that as long as Douglass and other black leaders seemed to show a greater respect for white leaders than their own, Afro-Americans would accomplish very little.

Delany's criticism of cooperation between Douglass and Stowe sparked a debate in Douglass's newspaper. In an editorial, Douglass expressed his disagreement with his friend on the current predicament of black leaders. To him, Afro-Americans were neither self-sufficient nor independent. Until they were, it was pure folly for them to refuse any help from white sympathizers. Moreover, if black leaders lacked initiative and forthrightness, Delany was no better. Douglass noted that Delany spent considerable time and energy urging Afro-Americans to determine their own destinies, but that his overtures for black nationalism largely were ignored in black communities. Douglass concluded that Delany did not have a plan that was worthy of consideration. Anticipating such objections to his position, Delany declared, "I am aware, that I differ with many in thus expressing myself [referring to his lack of confidence in white antislavery leaders], but I cannot help it; though I stand alone, and offend my best friends, so help me god! in a matter of such moment and importance, I will express my opinion."

Neither Douglass nor any other moderate black leader could deter Delany from attacking white abolitionists, particularly Harriet Beecher

Stowe. He saw her as a definite danger to the cause of black self-determination. Even though she wrote about the sufferings of a slave in *Uncle Tom's Cabin*, she did not necessarily have great empathy for American blacks or for the African race as a whole. To Delany, she was an enemy because she approved of the "dependent colonizationist settlement of Liberia" and scoffed at the independent black Republic of Haiti.[12] In 1852 Delany saw Liberia as a black subservient state created by proslavery forces, with the assistance of antislavery advocates. He did not make any distinction between these two groups in the American Colonization Society, but placed both of them in that category of whites who perpetuated the involuntary emigration of Afro-Americans to Liberia. Furthermore, he felt that Stowe typified white paternalism. But Afro-Americans could overcome such influences by realizing that "[their] elevation must be the result of self-efforts, and the work of [their] own hands. No other human power can accomplish it."[13]

Delany asserted that a cultural awakening among Afro-Americans was the necessary prerequisite to independent action. He believed many blacks were not motivated to campaign for their full share of equality because they lacked a proper knowledge of their own role in American history; they needed to view the history of the United States from an Afro-American perspective. Their inferior status did not reflect the contribution their forefathers had made to the development of America: black men had shed their blood in the American Revolution and the War of 1812, and even as slaves Afro-Americans fostered the country's growth. From the black labor pool came the "bone and sinews" of the southern economy, which permitted a white leisure class to emerge in that section of the nation. Thus, the social ostracism they endured was a poor way to repay them.

Delany saw blacks in America as a cultural entity. They were Africans who had been divested of their original cultural traits while in slavery. They were subjected to an acculturative process which transformed them into Anglo-Africans. Despite this conversion from Africans to Afro-Americans, however, the black race in the United States had the potential for nationhood. Like subject peoples in Europe such as the Poles, Hungarians, or Jews, Delany remarked, black men also yearned for "the day when they may return to their former national position of self-government and independence, let that be in whatever part of the habitable world it may."[14] As a keen observer of the nationalist movements in Europe in the late 1840s, Delany hoped to see Afro-Americans inspired by their own cultural nationalism.

By the end of 1852 Delany had one goal: to encourage black emigrationists to find some place in the world where they could determine their own destiny and contribute to the building of new black states. He said, "Our cause is a just one; the greatest at present that elicits the attention of the world. . . . Our race is to be redeemed; it is a great and glorious work, and we are the instrumentalities by which it is to be done. But we must go from among our oppressors; it never can be done by staying among them."[15] To accomplish the task that lay before them, emigrationists would have to be bold enough to venture out on their own and learn to endure many hardships to achieve their purpose, and they should plan to go to areas of the world where there was a substantial nonwhite population. In 1852, Delany accordingly espoused emigration to Central America, South America, and the West Indies—preferably the West Indies.

It was not unusual for emigrationists to favor settlement in the Western Hemisphere because of the sizable black population in many countries there. Brazil had a large number of former slaves, many of whom were Yoruba in origin. Like many people in his time and since, Delany subscribed to the view that the Portuguese treatment of Africans was not as horrendous as the treatment of Afro-Americans in the United States. Until Liberia was established in 1821, only Ethiopia and the Republic of Haiti had credibility for Afro-Americans. Moreover, by 1833 the British government had abolished slavery in its empire, which included many island possessions in the West Indies. After that year many Afro-Americans emigrated to the West Indies in search of a freer existence than in the United States. Between 1834 and 1840 at least 360 Afro-Americans emigrated to Trinidad, and others moved to Jamaica before 1850.[16]

Perhaps the boldest aspect of Delany's call for emigration to the Western Hemisphere was his view that men of the black diaspora could build viable states in an area of the world where European colonialism had been entrenched so firmly since the sixteenth century. One white critic of Delany's movement argued that any weakening of European dominance in Latin America and the Caribbean would be an impossible task for the black emigrationists. Furthermore, blacks would have to move quickly because American preeminence was rapidly replacing European colonialism in the hemisphere. The important point to note here is not that Delany pressed for schemes that seemed impractical because black men lacked the power to achieve them, but that he dared to challenge the concept of European imperialism in the 1850s.

Convinced that his emphasis on black self-determinism was just, that the time was right for him and his supporters to seek a permanent home elsewhere, Delany prepared to unite all of the emigrationists in the United States and Canada. At his home in Pittsburgh in 1853, Delany drafted the *Call* for a national emigration convention, which met in Cleveland, Ohio, 24–26 August 1854. Although Douglass was against emigrationism, he advertised the announcement for the conference from the fall of 1853 until the eve of the Cleveland conclave. It was publicized also in the black newspaper in Chatham, Ontario, the *Provincial Freeman*.[17]

If there was any hope of resolving the conflict among black leaders on the issue of emigration, such optimism was dashed to the ground when the 1853 Afro-American convention at Rochester, New York, emphatically declared its opposition to all colonization and emigration schemes, black or white.[18] From then on emigrationists were convinced there could be no reconciliation between them and their more moderate contemporaries. This rebuttal of Delany and his supporters was largely responsible for the restrictive nature of the emigration convention. Only black men who favored emigration would be allowed to attend the Cleveland meeting; however, Delany hoped to attract participants from throughout the Western Hemisphere, including the West Indies and Mexico. It would be a meeting of black men with a single interest and goal, making Delany's 1854 convention a unique happening in the annals of Afro-American history in the nineteenth century.

In the *Call* Delany made it emphatically clear that emigration would be the only topic discussed in Cleveland. Emigrationists had to decide *where* to go. Even on this cardinal point, however, the options for discussion were limited. The elimination of Asia and Europe as possible areas for black emigration did not require an explanation but the exclusion of Liberia did. Delany did not want black migrants to travel there because of the work of the American Colonization Society, his avowed enemy. In the *Call* Delany clarified the reason for the exclusion: "Colonizationists are advised that no favors will be shown to them or their expatriating scheme, as we have no sympathy with the enemies of our race."[19] Delany's nationalism was so firmly rooted he would not accept a scheme that came under the auspices of white American philanthropists. On the other hand, the work of the ACS in Liberia did not lessen his appreciation of Africa and Africans.

While Douglass published Delany's *Call* for the Cleveland convention in his newspaper, he did nothing or said nothing to encourage the growth of emigrationism. His stance typified the general antipathy of Afro-Americans toward leaving North America. If Douglass and others in America exhibited pessimism about the emigrationists, there was more optimism in Canada, especially in the stance taken by another black editor, Mary Ann Shadd. She believed that the black community in Chatham, Ontario, represented what blacks could accomplish outside of the United States. There were some black business enterprises in the town, and she visualized a multiplication of such establishments if Delany's movement succeeded. Like him, she felt emigrationists would demonstrate the proper way for New World blacks to progress.

Undaunted by opposition to the *Call*, the emigrationists met in Cleveland on 24–25 August 1854. Delegates came from eight northern states, three southern states, and Ontario. All together, from 1200 to 1500 persons attended the plenary sessions and 200 participated in the executive sessions.[20] Not only were the numbers who attended the emigration convention impressive, when compared to those who attended other black conferences in the first half of the nineteenth century, but Delany also had the support of some of the more prominent black abolitionists at the time. Among those who were selected as state commissioners for the national organization were William C. Nell and Charles Lenox Remond of Massachusetts and Rev. William C. Monroe of Detroit, Michigan. The large number who attended and the black leaders who aligned themselves with Delany's cause seemed to indicate that some Afro-Americans entertained notions of emigration when the threat of the Fugitive Slave Law caused widespread anxiety.

At the very beginning of the convention, it appeared as though Delany might not be selected as the titular head of the movement he initiated. Black clergymen were elected to most of the executive positions. Rev. Monroe of Detroit was named president, and among the four vice presidents were Bishop William Paul Quinn of Indiana and Rev. William J. Fuller of Rhode Island; Rev. James T. Holly was one of the three secretaries. Delany, however, was appointed chairman of the Business Committee. Since clergymen were the nucleus of black leadership in the nineteenth century, it was not unusual that they filled many of the key positions. Nonetheless, Delany was not about to relinquish the pivotal role of his movement to these traditional leaders. The Business Committee became the policy-making body for the emigrationists.

The Business Commitee drafted the "Platform: or Decalaration of Sentiments of the Cleveland Convention," which bore the imprint of Delany's nationalistic ideas. In this document the emigrationists clearly stated the reasons for their disenchantment with America, their disgust with black and white abolitionists, and their "blueprint" for black upward mobility. In the first instance, they held that black people in America had waited unavailingly for their "white fellow countrymen" to apply the doctrine of equality. The men in Cleveland believed the Constitution of the United States was a spurious document because it allowed an "unrestricted liberty" only to whites and upheld "slavery and degradation" for black people. Furthermore, the conventioneers argued that all political parties in the country approved of the racial dichotomy in the nation's most sacred document. Such institutional racism provided partial justification for planning to leave the United States. The emigrationists also felt they could not overlook the series of political compromises in the 1840s and 1850s which greatly proscribed Afro-American rights; specifically, they cited the Missouri Compromise, the Fugitive Slave Law, and the Kansas-Nebraska Bill.

Although emigrationists had reached the conclusion that there could be no unity of black and white interests, they nonetheless believed in "the natural equality of the Human Race." They therefore had to oppose any effort which did not further true democracy, regardless of its source. Consequently, while Douglass and other black leaders were encouraged greatly because Afro-Americans voted in some northern states, emigrationists debunked such token gains. According to their seventh plank, no black man was free until all had "the right of self-representation."[21] Lack of participation in government provided the emigrationists with yet another reason for flight from America; they sought a polity where they could vote and hold office.

Finally, in their platform, the emigrationists implied that the main prerequisites for black improvement were an adequate but varied education and racial solidarity. They admonished black people throughout the world to educate themselves and their children in technological, scientific, professional, and agricultural fields; then they could compete with and demand an equal place in the world. To complement their educational base, blacks had to avoid a self-imposed social and cultural stratification. They had to see themselves as one class of people and, whether referred to as Negroes, Africans, Blacks, Coloreds, or Mulattoes, nurture a pride for their race.[22] Hence, pan-Africanist sentiment was an integral part of the ideology of the emigrationists. As Afro-Americans they viewed themselves as only one part of the black universe; from this perspective, they dedicated themselves to the realization of world-wide black solidarity.

Every social or political movement makes preparations to publicize its doctrines and goals, and the emigrationists were no exception to this general rule. James M. Whitfield, Holly, and William Lambert presented a proposal to the convention for the establishment of a quarterly periodical that would serve two functions: to disseminate information about the emigrationists and their activities, and to publish relevant scholarly articles. This innovation represented a significant departure because until 1854, none of the Afro-American conventions had established a black journal. Until the proposed journal was published, however, the emigrationists decided to publicize their activities in William Howard Day's newspaper in Cleveland, Ohio, the *Aliened American*. They ruled out the use of *Frederick Douglass' Paper* because of his denunciation of their movement (see Appendix A for a copy of the proposed journal). The differences between the moderate black leaders and the radical emigrationists explained this new development. To achieve a national posture for black people, the radicals believed it imperative to offset the prejudicial and stereotypical views of black history and progress expressed in the writings of white authors. Delany's group contended there were enough black intellectuals in America to present an objective appraisal of the attainments of the race. Furthermore, a journal might provide them with an "inducement to write."

If there was any doubt that Delany would be appointed head of the movement, it was dispelled when the convention drafted its *Constitution of the National Board of Commissioners*. Delany enjoyed a definite political advantage at the convention. Power was in the hands of the executive delegates from eleven states and Canada. Two thirds of the 139 delegates came from the Pittsburgh area, which gave Delany an overwhelming advantage in the deliberations of the convention.

The constitution was designed to locate the headquarters and executive officers near the home of the president of the National Board. Since Delany was chosen as president, the administrative center for the emigration movement from 1854 to 1856 was Pittsburgh. The executive department consisted of the president, vice president, secretary, treasurer, auditor, and special foreign secretary, of whom the first five were residents of Pittsburgh.[23] The constitution also created committees for domestic, financial, and foreign relations. In drafting the constitution with Rev. William Webb, Delany ensured that the future activities and organization of the emigrationists would have a nationalistic emphasis. Article 21 stated that the National Board of Commissioners and subsequent conventions would operate "on the basis of the Cleveland Platform, and principles of a Black Nationality."[24]

Before the end of the Cleveland convention, Delany delivered the keynote address entitled "The Political Destiny of the Colored Race." While he reiterated many of his earlier views on emigrationism and black nationality, he implored his compatriots to actualize an emigration program immediately because of impending changes in the international arena. Delany had anticipated the imperialism of the late nineteenth century and the ensuing lengthy conflict between Europe and the Third World. Long before W. E. B. DuBois, Delany postulated the view that the struggle in the future would be between the white and darker races of the world. He said, "It would be duplicity longer to disguise the fact, that the great issue, sooner or later, upon which must be disputed the world's destiny, will be a question of black and white; and every individual will be called upon for his identity with one or the other. The blacks and colored races are four-sixths of all the population of the world: and these people are fast tending to a common cause with each other."[25] Delany admonished Afro-Americans to prepare for an active role in the inevitable racial struggle. Emigration to areas of the world where black men resided was one way of checking European hegemony. In this context, however, Delany revealed the essential flaw in his otherwise rigid black nationalism. He did not see all white men, especially not Englishmen, as enemies of his race, because, at the moment, he felt that the English would help the emigrationists. Delany knew the United Kingdom was the chief perpetrator of the Atlantic slave trade, but it had redeemed itself by being the first European nation to abolish slavery in its colonial possessions. In addition, antislavery men in the British Isles were willing to aid downtrodden Afro-Americans.

Although Delany's speech reflected his radical views on black progress, it also revealed his flexibility of thought about world-sites for emigration. He always had a personal preference for Africa, but the majority of the emigrationists preferred to seek a haven closer to home, and Delany yielded to this preference. In his address, he provided them with much information about the West Indies and Central and South America—information he had been collecting since the 1830s. Delany considered tropical areas to be ideal because of their large black and brown populations; he believed Afro-Americans would have a better chance of participating in the cultural, economic, and social life among dark-skinned people than among the Anglo-Saxons of North America. If they could not go to Latin America or the West Indies immediately, Delany advised them to move to Canada. Since the enactment of the Fugitive Slave Law, however, Delany feared that Canada might be annexed by the United States and made slave territory. Hence, he planned ultimately to take emigrants from Canada to Africa.

Although emigrationists appeared optimistic about escaping from white oppression in America, they could not avoid the omnipresent, passionate criticism of their movement by moderate black leaders. From the first announcement of the *Call*, moderate black leaders launched a campaign to discredit emigrationism in northern black communities. Frederick Douglass led the attack on Delany's movement by defining it as a divisive cause that was "uncalled for, unwise, unfortunate, and premature."[26] Because of his opposition, Delany and William Howard Day, editor of the *Aliened American*, claimed Douglass purposely printed an incomplete copy of the *Call* in his newspaper.[27] Douglass retorted that Delany could hardly accuse him of being unfair when only emigrationist sympathizers would be allowed to attend the Cleveland convention.

Delany's movement increased apprehension among moderate Afro-American leaders about colonization. To counter mounting anxiety, A. D. Jenkins argued that a national convention should have been called to denounce black emigrationists and white colonizationists; to make it known that an overwhelming black majority intended to make the United States "the battleground of . . . liberation." Moreover, if emigrationists wanted to quit America, they should leave quietly and not convey the discordant impression that large numbers of black people wanted to emigrate.[28]

Moderate black leaders also objected to the radical ideology of the emigrationists. Specifically, they disapproved of the view that Afro-Americans could not achieve equality in America. William J. Watkins, an associate of Douglass, thought emigrationist leaders were too pessimistic. He admitted that Afro-Americans were not accorded equal status, but there was a ray of hope. He referred to Massachusetts, where black men had some rights by law, and thus joined the community that ruled in the United States. Delany's argument that Afro-Americans were a nation within a nation was therefore erroneous. Douglass argued that, despite origins, black Americans were not aliens and had every right to remain in the country and work for equality. Although the door to democracy hardly was ajar in the 1850s, black moderates believed it eventually would swing open. Thus, Afro-Americans should not seek democracy elsewhere but wait in their homeland until it came to them.

On the point of a black nation, John I. Gaines of Cincinnati doubted whether Delany and Whitfield were correct when they claimed that Afro-Americans would gain greater respect from white men if they constructed a viable nation. For example, he did not see how black men received more respect because of the existence of Haiti and Liberia. White men only respected power, and since these black nations had none, the formation of another weak state would be counterproductive. Instead, blacks should follow the guidelines of the Rochester Convention; by improving themselves intellectually and economically in America they would achieve an elevated position. In comparing the moderate and emigrationist positions, Gaines believed the Rochester Convention represented light, truth, wisdom, and a practical program for Afro-American progress, whereas the emigrationists represented darkness, error, weakness, and misdirection. The moderates also believed that few blacks would leave America under the aegis of the emigrationists, and they would not be able to build a nation anywhere.

The charge that irritated the emigrationists most was Douglass's reference to them as irresponsible men. He accused them of running away from the struggle to help their enslaved brothers. Whitfield, one of the leading emigrationists, claimed that the desire for a free existence in another nation was not unlike Douglass's escape to the North where he joined the antislavery cause. Delany's reaction to this charge of irresponsibility was stronger than that of Whitfield. He said, "it is not all who talk the loudest about staying here for the sake of the slave, who love him or his cause most, or even at all."[30] He saw moderates as part of a growing black elite who would not help a fugitive slave, and who preferred to live among whites. Thus Delany was not shaken by the charge that emigrationists were really escapists; he was not deterred from a more nationalistic course of action.

The attack of black moderate leaders on the emigration movement was indicative of the well-nigh universal disdain Afro-Americans held for causes that would take large numbers of them from America. They seemed to feel that the advocacy of such schemes by a group of black men was even more treacherous than their promotion by whites. The latter case was explicable given the prejudicial attitudes prevalent in nineteenth-century America, but for black men to openly advocate emigrationism was treasonable. Delany's movement therefore caused far greater polarization among black leaders of the time than any other single issue. Once the emigrationists became more noticeable in 1853, moderate leaders did not stop to make fine distinctions between them and white colonizationists. They saw both groups as schemers who planned to deprive Afro-Americans of the right to rise in the country of their birth. Despite the opposition, however, Delany did not relent. In 1854, he and his followers launched a new movement that challenged both black and white abolitionist leaders.

4

From Emigrationist to Pan-Africanist

Before the Cleveland Convention ended, two other emigration enthusiasts emerged to share the leadership with Delany: Rev. James T. Holly and James M. Whitfield, both of whom were the New York state delegates to the convention. Holly had associated with emigrationists in Ontario between 1851 and 1853. He noted that the 1854 Cleveland Convention was a watershed in the life of Delany, who thereafter dedicated himself completely to the pursuit of a nationalistic course.[1] Whitfield was a barber in Buffalo who had advocated black emigrationism since 1838. He dedicated a book of poems to Delany because he "admired his character, . . . talents, and . . . his principles."[2] Although all three men were staunch emigrationists, they differed about where blacks should go. But the convention avoided a clash between them with this declaration:

> The Board shall appoint a Foreign Commission, to consist of not more than three persons, whose business it shall be to go on a Foreign Mission, to such countries and places as they may be instructed; to make a geographical, topographical and political enquiry into the state and condition of those places and people; who shall hold correspondence with the Committee of Foreign Relations, whenever convenient; provided that in their official duties, the position of the colored people in the United States be not compromised, and their mission does not exceed one year.[3]

This provision allowed each man to go to the part of the world he preferred for Afro-American emigration, fully reconnoiter the country and its people, and report his findings to a biannual emigration meeting. Those who intended to emigrate could go to one of three locations:

with Delany to some portion of Africa, with Holly to Haiti, or with Whitfield to Central America.

Although the Cleveland Convention commissioned the "big three" to visit their respective areas of interest and return with the appropriate information, Delany, Holly, and Whitfield found it difficult to execute their plans because they could not overcome the problems they encountered. Holly first went on a reconnaissance mission. He visited Haiti at his own expense in 1855, but its government was not receptive to his emigration scheme at that time.[4] Four years later, however, Haiti appointed a white man, James Redpath, as its emigration agent in the United States. This circumstance did not deter Holly and many other Afro-Americans from emigrating to Haiti in the early 1860s.

The emigrationists could not raise sufficient funds to pay for Whitfield's journey to Central America. They became so destitute they compromised with principle and sought support for Whitfield from a colonizationist. At the time, Congressman Frances Preston Blair, a Free-Soiler from Missouri, who advocated gradual emancipation through the deportation and resettlement of Afro-Americans, urged the federal government to establish a colonization scheme for Central America. Whitfield and Holly wrote to Blair about the black emigration movement and its plans to send a group to Central America, providing money was available. Even if the United States government had allocated funds, Whitfield's Central American project ended prematurely when he died in California.[5]

In addition to a lack of funds to realize their goals, emigrationists experienced other frustrations. For instance, Delany hoped to internationalize his movement, in line with his view of a world-wide partnership among black people. Shortly after the 1854 convention Delany accordingly corresponded with a prominent black Jamaican politician, Edward Jordon, and asked for his assistance in organizing a hemisphere-wide convention on emigration. At that time, Jordon was a legislative member of Jamaica's ruling Town Party and an editor of the *Kingston Journal*.[8] Jordon responded that it presently was unwise to plan such an event because of the political conflict in Jamaica between West Indians and British officials over the franchise. Delany was not satisfied with his reply and classified Jordon as a former black champion who had grown soft with time.[6]

Even if Jordon had agreed to work with Delany for solidarity in the hemisphere, it is doubtful whether they could have persuaded large numbers of Afro-Americans to go to the British West Indies in the 1850s. When the British passed the Emancipation Act of 1833, many West Indian planters had to search elsewhere for laborers. By the 1840s the problem was serious enough for the Jamaican government to send an emigration agent, Alexander Barclay, to the United States and Canada to persuade Afro-Americans to settle there, but only 427 Afro-Americans emigrated to Jamaica between 1840 and 1845. Most refused to go because the standard of living was lower there than in the northern states. Simultaneously, there seemed to be little encouragement from countries in South and Central America for Delany's movement.[7]

By 1856, Delany was fully aware of the opposition at home and abroad to black emigrationism. After two years of searching for moral and financial support among black men in and out of the United States, Delany decided to reorient his movement. By doing so, he purposely drifted away from an emphasis on black solidarity in the Western Hemisphere and began to develop ideas for a more concerted pan-Africanism. Once Delany decided to follow the impulse of his "first love," Africa, he created a dilemma for his own movement. He had compromised with those colleagues who insisted on staying close to the United States, and he encouraged Holly and Whitfield to realize their goals, but he failed to provide them with the main essential, money. If Delany was to accomplish his own goal, he had to move quickly because he was forty-four years old. Thus, in 1856 Delany chartered one course, a back-to-Africa scheme. Although he did not deliberately deny Holly and Whitfield his support, his dedication to an African-oriented goal caused him to channel the remaining resources of black emigrationism into his own program.

First, Delany moved his headquarters and his family to Chatham, Ontario, where he began to practice medicine. Mary Ann Shadd, the leading emigrationist advocate in Western Ontario, urged the black citizenry to patronize the skilled physician, who charged modest fees.[8] Delany undoubtedly selected Chatham because many black people from Pittsburgh had migrated there earlier in the 1850s, and he had the support of the *Provincial Freeman*. As the main Ontario terminus of the underground railroad in 1850, Chatham had a black population of 2000, one-third of the total population of the town.[9] Moreover, as sectional conflict grew in the United States, the number of Afro-American emigrants increased. In Chatham, Delany hoped to find new moral and financial support for his back-to-Africa scheme.

From his new residence, Delany summoned emigrationists to their first biannual meeting in August 1856, at the African Methodist Episcopal Church in Cleveland, Ohio. The convention hoped to generate new interest in emigrationism by making substantive changes in its program and reorganizing the Board of Commissioners. Delany was reelected president of the Board, and H. Ford Douglas, an editor of the *Provincial Freeman*, was appointed as agent and lecturer for the convention. The publication of the *Afro-American Repository* was also reaffirmed in 1856. Most of all, the emigrationists tried to solve their financial dilemma by forming a joint-stock company called the North American-West Indian Trading Association. Its stocks would cost $50 per share, and the money would be used to exploit trade between the United States and the West Indies. Because of illness, Delany was not able to attend the 1856 biannual meeting, but from the convention deliberations it was obvious that emigrationists still saw him as the guiding spirit for their movement, and they were optimistic about the realization of their goals.

During the interval between the first and second biannual emigration conventions (1856–1858), Delany continued to formulate his plans to go to Africa, but he simultaneously plunged into the politics of Kent County, Ontario. Delany became the key black campaigner for a local politician, Archie McKellar, who sought a seat in the Ontario Provincial Parliament. Although Delany achieved some success in the McKellar campaign, he experienced defeat in the municipal elections of late 1857. He was one of the leaders of the Committee of Colored Voters which sent a petition to Chatham's Municipal Council 7 December 1857 asking it to name a black man to the three-man Board of Assessors for Chatham.[10] The council refused, arguing that the white assessors served everyone. If they did not, black inhabitants had the right of appeal.[11]

Following his political activism in Chatham, Delany faced a new challenge that could have diverted him from his pan-African goal. By 1858, John Brown hoped to gain support from black leaders in the United States and Canada for his grandiose schemes to end slavery in the South. Unable to obtain any commitment from Frederick Douglass, he turned to Delany in Canada, but at an inopportune time. Delany had his own problems: he was busy persuading his emigrationist colleagues to send him to Africa. However, he did help Brown to organize a convention in Chatham in the spring of 1858.[12]

Brown was unable to obtain a total commitment from Delany because their goals were incompatible. While Brown thought of forming a state consisting largely of blacks within the continental boundaries of the United States, Delany believed black men needed to leave America and join with their brethren elsewhere to build black nations. Moreover, given his philosophy, Delany would not associate himself with any scheme which a white man would lead. In any case, he could not afford to align himself too closely with Brown, who had not been well received by blacks in Western Ontario. Many did not know who he was,[13] and Rev. William King and Josiah Henson portrayed Brown as an interloper who would do them more harm than good. Delany could not alienate these leaders, especially King, because he planned to take people from the Elgin Settlement in Buxton, Ontario, to Africa.

Before his own 1858 convention met in Chatham, four months after John Brown's, Delany gradually built up support for his scheme to take black men from the North American continent to Africa. First of all, he began to correspond with Sierra Leonians in Yorubaland (Western Nigeria) and claimed that he had received favorable replies about the possibilities of visiting that part of West Africa.[14] Second, the back-to-Africa protagonist consulted with some Afro-American intellectuals about his plans, and they also responded favorably. The reaction of Wisconsin black emigrationists was particularly encouraging because they appointed Jonathan J. Myers to consult with Delany about his scheme, and they endorsed it. Robert Douglass, the prominent black artist of Philadelphia, recommended that he take the Jamaican chemist Robert Campbell with him. M. H. Freeman, an advocate of emigration, supported Delany and regretted not having gone to West Africa (Liberia) himself when he was much younger. With this moral support from black contemporaries on both sides of the Atlantic, Delany proceeded to make the emigration movement conform to his pan-Africanism.

The emigrationists met at Chatham, Ontario, from the fourth to the seventh of August in 1858 for the third time. At this meeting changes crucial to Delany's plans to go to Africa were made in both the constitution and goals of the movement. Initially, the convention changed the personnel of the executive department so that the chief officials would be residents of Western Ontario. In the reorganization of the Board of Commissioners, William Howard Day became president, and Delany was appointed foreign secretary. In the new capacity Delany insisted that the name of the organization be changed to reflect a universal interest in black people. The emigrationists partly acceded to their leader's request by amending their constitution to change the name Emigration Convention to the Association for the Promotion of the Interest of the Colored People of Canada and the United States. The new title suggested that Delany had compromised with his fellow emigrationists. He definitely wanted a stated commitment to Africa, but his colleagues were reluctant. However, as with the opposition from without, Delany did not let the objections from within deter him from his African dream.

As the new president of the emigrationists, William Howard Day expressed his objections to a more African-oriented movement. Although on the periphery of emigrationism in 1854, Day decided to become an integral part of the movement after he moved to Dresden, Ontario, in 1856. At the Chatham convention he made it clear he was going to devote his energies to unity among the black émigré's in Canada and the enfranchisement of Afro-Americans. The emigrationists were faced with an unpleasant task in Chatham. Few of them really shared Delany's dedication to a regenerated Africa; most continued to think in terms of emigration in the Western Hemisphere. However, they could not overlook their moral responsibility to a leader whose nationalism was rooted in a strong attachment to Africa. In 1858 the emigrationists reluctantly agreed to let Delany go to Africa to gather data that would substantiate his arguments about the motherland's great potential for Afro-American settlement.

To make Delany's reconnaissance mission to Africa possible the new "Association" commissioned him to head the Niger Valley Exploring Party. The men Delany selected to accompany him were Robert Campbell, J. W. Purnell, Robert Douglass, and Amos Aray. Some of the men at the convention questioned Delany's choice of Robert Campbell, a West Indian, who was not an active emigrationist. But Delany explained that Campbell was dedicated to their principles. Satisfied with Delany's explanation, the convention accepted Campbell and the other three men as official members of the exploring party. If Delany was elated when the Executive Council promulgated the objectives of the Niger Valley Exploring Party on 31 August 1858 the very language of the document revealed the internal conflict between Delany and the conservatives in his movement. William Howard Day, Isaac D. Shadd, and George W. Brodie made it clear that while emigrationists supported the scientific aspects of Delany's expedition to Africa, they were "entirely opposed to any Emigration there as such."[15] The members of the exploring party could make separate arrangements for Afro-Americans to go to Africa if they wished to do so, but the emigrationists would not pay for such schemes. The contradiction between Delany and his movement typified the problems he encountered eight months before he embarked for Africa in 1859.

Shortly after the Executive Council publicized Delany's mission to Africa, the commissioners of the Niger Valley Exploring Party visited northern cities—New York, Boston, and Philadelphia—to raise funds for their journey to Africa. Delany sought aid only from people who tolerated his pan-Africanism, but Campbell and Purnell were willing to take money from colonizationists. They went to the headquarters of the American Colonization Society in Washington, D.C., to solicit funds from its executive committee, but it refused to help them.[16] However, colonizationist opposition to emigrationism was not universal. Joseph Tracy of the Massachusetts Colonization Society was against Delany's movement because it was not directed toward Liberia, but J. B. Pinney of the New York Colonization Society and William Coppinger of the Pennsylvania Colonization Society favored it. Coppinger argued that the American Colonization Society financially was able to contribute $500 to $1000 to Delany's Yorubaland scheme. Pinney contended that colonizationist support of emigration may have encouraged more highly skilled Afro-Americans to emigrate to Liberia. Furthermore, if some Liberians accompanied Delany to Yorubaland, it would extend the influence of the new Republic and the society to another part of West Africa, and keep the migrationists from seeking aid in Britain. Because of these interests in Delany's movement, his good reputation as a resident of Philadelphia, and his determination, the Pennsylvania Colonization Society gave Campbell $60 toward his passage to England and Africa. Campbell hoped to raise another $300 in England for the Exploring Party's journey to Yorubaland.[17]

Because the Niger Valley Exploring Party was unable to raise sufficient funds to pay all of their expenses to Africa, Delany altered his plans. Since he and Campbell were the only commissioners who had received enough money to begin the journey to Yorubaland, Delany reluctantly dropped Douglass, Purnell, and Aray from the party. Delany claimed his movement suffered because northern colonizationists had launched a campaign to thwart his African scheme; they had maligned his character and purposely sent false information to Britain about his intentions. Delany directed his remarks mainly to colonizationists in Philadelphia from whom Campbell had received financial support. He felt that they had tried deliberately to create tensions between himself and his West Indian partner. Writing two years later, the leader of the Niger Valley Exploring Party asserted that he had not authorized Campbell to consort with colonizationists, but admitted his indebtedness to Campbell for the initiative he took in obtaining money from some of them.[18]

Delany's suspicions about white opposition to his African scheme were correct. For instance, while William Coppinger provided Campbell with funds for his journey to Africa, he did not want the commissioners of the Niger Valley Exploring Party to travel to Africa in ships carrying Afro-Americans to Liberia for the American Colonization Society, because of Delany's declared independence from colonizationists. Moreover, J. B. Pinney concluded that Delany and Campbell received little financial support in America because white men had no confidence in a movement led by blacks and colonizationists refused to believe both men were serious about their enterprise until they actually left for Africa. By early April the two commissioners realized they would not collect any more money in America and decided to leave for Africa with the little they had. On 23 April 1859, Campbell left for England where he planned to solicit funds from Britons sympathetic to Delany's movement.[19] Shortly after Campbell departed, Delany obtained some donations from wellwishers in New York, and began his journey to Africa on 24 May. The pan-African advocate said he embarked for Africa "for the Promotion of the political and other interests of the colored people of the United States and the Canadas."[20] He was obsessed with the idea that black men on both sides of the Atlantic collectively could build viable enterprises without the help of white philanthropy. However, Delany soon learned that the supporters Campbell had found would have a definite influence on his intended goals, if not his ideology.

Delany's trip to Africa was the initial step in the realization of a hoped-for Afro-American-African enterprise that he had been thinking about for fourteen years. Although originally a black emigrationist, Delany consistently drifted toward becoming a confirmed pan-Africanist. By 1852, Africa had become the focal point of his thoughts. His romantic attachment to the continent and its history was very strong. He revered its past and conceived of ways he could participate in its regeneration. Delany contended that re-emergence of the continent to prominence would come primarily through economic development, and from 1845 to 1859 he had thought about various growth schemes.

In 1845 he had postulated the view that Afro-Americans and Africans could build a thriving commercial base on the northeast coast of Africa near the Horn. This entrepot would become the eastern juncture of a trans-African railroad that would link the west coast of the continent with the east coast. As the railroad traversed Central Africa, it would pick up mineral ores to transport to a West African port. In this way Africans and Afro-Americans could take advantage of the trade going from the Far East to Europe and America. Delany apparently was unconcerned about the political and cultural heterogeneity of African peoples residing along the proposed route, whose consent he would have to obtain to make his grand scheme a success. Similar to European "dreamers of empire" in the nineteenth century, Delany constantly kept the end in view and overlooked any detailed consideration of the cost of achieving his goal.

While Delany's *Project for an Expedition of Adventure to the Eastern Coast of Africa* may be viewed as far-fetched, it reflected his pan-Africanism. Basically, Delany visualized men from the black diaspora working with Africans to develop the natural resources of the continent. Although he gave up hope of the realization of his transcontinental scheme, in 1859 he felt that cooperation between Old and New World blacks was possible in Yorubaland. The pan-African advocate believed Africans and Afro-Americans could build a modern state in West Africa whose economic vitality would attract world-wide attention. Thus buried deep in Delany's 1845 scheme was the rudimentary idea of a new nationalism founded on the common needs and aspirations of Africans and Afro-Americans.

As European missionaries and explorers penetrated the interior of the African continent by the 1850s, Delany eagerly read their works to enhance his knowledge of Africa. Many Afro-Americans were intrigued with David Livingstone's exploits in Central and East Africa, but Delany was more interested in European and American activities in that portion of West Africa now known as Nigeria. From the journals of Dixon Denham, Hugh Clapperton, and Richard L. Lander, he learned about some of the cultural aspects of the Hausa-Fulani peoples who were the northern "neighbors" of the Yorubas.[21]

More specifically, from the writings of Thomas Jefferson Bowen, an American missionary for the Southern Baptist Convention, Delany was able to obtain primary information of the people living in Yorubaland. Bowen labored in Yorubaland from 1849 to 1854, but he only made one African convert and did not establish a mission station there until 1854.[22] Because he traveled extensively through Yorubaland during this six-year period, Bowen was able to give a personal description of the people and the area of West Africa in which they lived. It is easy to see why Delany was intrigued by Bowen's book. The missionary wrote optimistically about the regeneration of Africa, and he believed that Afro-Americans and repatriated Africans could play a major role in the acceleration of commercial and missionary activities in the Niger basin. In fact, because of Bowen's glowing reports to the American Colonization Society about Yorubaland, the society considered establishing another colony of Afro-Americans there, but the sectional antagonism at home and the hostility of Yoruba chiefs to missionaries prevented its fruition.

While Bowen thought in terms of another "Liberia" for Yorubaland, Delany thought in terms of an independent nation. Instead of merely establishing another colony of Afro-Americans subsidized by American philanthropy, Delany believed that in Yorubaland he would see the realization of his dream of black men from America and Africa working together to build a viable economy.

When Delany boarded the *Mendi* in the spring of 1859, he began a new episode in his life that had originated from his experiences in America and the way in which he reacted to them as a black man. From the 1840s he had become disenchanted with white abolitionists and the work of the American Colonization Society, and he disliked the moderate tendencies of the black leaders in the Afro-American convention movement. In addition, denied the opportunity to complete his medical training, and feeling that the proslavery forces in the nation would gain the advantage in the sectional crisis and further subjugate *all* Afro-Americans, he decided that it was time for black men in America to pursue a course of black nationalism.

Hoping to play the leading role in this new movement, Delany espoused the view that Afro-Americans must realize that their destiny was inextricably linked with black men in the West Indies and Africa. Hence he began his drive for emigrationism through which he hoped men from all three areas could cooperate to build the new black states of modern times. To placate those in his movement who preferred emigration to some part of the Western Hemisphere, he subdued his own desire to form stronger ties between Africans and Afro-Americans. But in 1856 when it was apparent that emigrationism would not succeed, he began to persuade some in his movement to put their full support behind his plan to go to Africa. Thus, his pan-African scheme for Yorubaland was to be the positive conclusion to a mainly negative emigration movement.

5

The Journey to Africa

From Mungo Park's exploration of the Niger River in 1788 until Britain's annexation of Lagos in 1861, English explorers, missionaries, and merchants developed a keen interest in Yorubaland, especially the town of Abeokuta. Abeokuta was the new homeland of the Egba people. Between 1825 and 1840 the Fulani of Hausaland (Northwestern Nigeria) invaded the Old Oyo empire in Yorubaland and destroyed many villages and towns. The war and destruction caused the Egba and other Yoruba groups to migrate southward. The Egba finally settled at Abeokuta, which becamse one of the principal towns in Southern Yorubaland by the 1850s. Missionaries focused their attention on Abeokuta because many repatriated Africans settled there after their rescue from slave ships and rehabilitation at Sierra Leone. The most ambitious missionary organization to work among the ex-slaves was the Church Missionary Society (CMS), whose missionaries hoped their African converts would help them to extend Christianity in Yorubaland.

During the 1850s and 1860s, English merchants tried to persuade the Egba people to mass-produce cotton. These traders believed that obtaining new cotton supplies from Yorubaland would serve two purposes. First, the trade would extend British influence beyond Lagos. Second, Yoruba cotton could be useful if events in the United States decreased supply. Consequently, some cotton merchants supported the work of the CMS in Yorubaland because they believed both Christianity and commerce contributed to the growth of legitimate trade between Africans and Europeans.

Delany's and Campbell's presence in Yorubaland in 1859 as commissioners of the Niger Valley Exploring Party drew varying reactions from local Europeans. Because of the inclination to associate Afro-American emigration with Liberia, English missionaries did not like the prospect of Delany bringing his countrymen to Yorubaland. On the other hand, Manchester cotton merchants believed that Delany's aims, if properly executed, would benefit their economic goals in Abeokuta. Thus, the Niger Valley Exploring Party's journey to Yorubaland was a challenge to British interests in that portion of West Africa. Furthermore, Delany and Campbell's travel beyond Lagos was significant for another reason. Exploration in Africa was considered to be the pursuit of Europeans, but the data the two commissioners collected became a vital part of the growing fund of knowledge about Yorubaland.

When Robert Campbell visited England in the early spring of 1859, he kept Delany's back-to-Africa movement from dying prematurely. Campbell discovered that many Britons were interested in black emigrationism, and he shrewdly appealed to them as a British subject from the New World. He told them that many of the black men who intended to go to Yorubaland resided in Canada. Henry Christy and Edmund Ashworth, antislavery advocates in London, were among those who agreed to help the Niger Valley Exploring Party. Christy already knew Delany; they had been introduced to each other in Canada in 1856 by John Scoble, then secretary of the London Anti-Slavery Society.[2] Among those in London who also helped Delany's cause were Dr. Thomas Hodgkin and Gerard Ralston. In addition to the financial support Campbell received from such interested persons in London, he was able to obtain aid from members of the Manchester Cotton Supply Association (MCSA). The organization was intrigued with Delany's African scheme because of its potential for adding to their sources of cotton. Primarily because of the economic possibilities of Delany's scheme, then, interested Britons and Campbell published a statement which urged people in England to aid the Niger Valley Exploring Party. Thus antislavery advocates and merchants in Britain helped Campbell to raise money for Delany's back-to-Africa movement.[2]

Delany's backers also persuaded the British Foreign Office to provide support. Cotton interests in Manchester asked the Earl of Malmesbury, the Secretary of State for Foreign Affairs, to provide Campbell and an Afro-American companion he met in England, John Bennett, with free passage from Liverpool to Lagos, and the secretary complied with their request. Once Campbell and future Afro-American emigrants reached Lagos, the Foreign Office agreed to give them the same assistance it provided to ex-slaves returning from Brazil and Cuba.[3]

The CMS was the only British group that disapproved of Delany's scheme. The Executive Secretary, Henry Venn, noted that when Campbell spoke to members of the Parent Committee in London they did not encourage him. Venn contended that Delany's effort to take Afro-Americans to Yorubaland was "visionary."[4] This apparent apprehension by leaders of the most prominent missionary organization working among the Egbas was symptomatic of later CMS opposition to Delany and Campbell in Abeokuta.

On 24 June 1859, Campbell left Liverpool for Lagos. During stopovers on the journey, he observed the diversity of West African towns. Writing about the trip a year later, Campbell concluded that Bathurst, with its wide streets and large houses, was the most developed town he had seen before reaching Nigeria. More than its physical appearance, however, Campbell seemed to be concerned mainly with relations between Africans and Europeans in an African setting. He saw only about thirty white persons at Bathurst, and he learned of another European settlement on McCarthy's Island further up the Gambia River, but he noted that the British used soldiers from their West Indian Regiment to protect both places. By way of contrast, Campbell witnessed a depressing scene at Freetown, Sierra Leone. Africans and Europeans were trying to return to a normal mode of living after smallpox and yellow fever had killed many of the townspeople. Several Sierra Leonians told Campbell that, in spite of the epidemic, there was considerable antagonism between black and white men in the town.

Perhaps Campbell's most eventful moment on the West African coast was spent at his next port of call, Cape Palmas, Liberia. During a three-hour stopover Campbell met Liberia's president, Stephen A. Benson, and Rev. Alexander Crummell, one of the country's most articulate advocates of Afro-American emigration to Africa. In his public lectures and sermons he frequently urged Afro-Americans to emigrate to Africa to work for its regeneration.[5] Crummell himself set the example. After he was graduated from Queens College, Cambridge University, in 1853, he moved to Liberia. There he became a prominent Episcopal clergyman, lecturer, and teacher for twenty years before he returned to the United States. Crummell took Campbell on a swift tour of Cape Palmas which included a visit to his church and school for boys. While at Cape Palmas, Campbell heard that Delany was at Monrovia. However, instead of trying to contact his partner at that time, he decided to continue his journey in accordance with their original plan to rendezvous at Lagos.[6]

Before arriving there, however, Campbell stopped at two points along the Gold Coast, Cape Coast and Accra. He considered the former an unattractive place where the harbor conditions were poor and clean water difficult to obtain. Accra, on the other hand, was a better port, where Campbell saw ample evidence of both Dutch and British influences; local African resentment of recently levied British taxes did not escape his attention. Such observations of the various West African towns and of the conditions of the indigenous people and their relations with Europeans became an essential part of the primary data collected by the commissioners of the Niger Valley Exploring Party. Campbell finally reached Lagos on 20 July 1859 and stayed there for six weeks as the guest of the British consul, Lodder.

As in England, Campbell appeared in Lagos at an opportune time. Here he met Sierra Leonians from Abeokuta who expressed a keen interest in Delany's movement. The most eager was Samuel Crowther, Jr., who was the son of one of the most prominent Sierra Leonians in Yorubaland in the nineteenth century, Rev. Samuel A. Crowther. Young Crowther and other Sierra Leonians told Campbell that the Egba authorities at Abeokuta would welcome black emigrants from America and Canada.[7] Because of his association with the younger Crowther, Campbell decided to accompany him to Abeokuta where he believed he could live more economically and collect additional information about the interior before Delany arrived.

Constantly aware of the mission of the Niger Valley Exploring Party, Campbell compiled economic data on the territory between Lagos and Abeokuta. He calculated the distance from Lagos to Abeokuta to be approximately ninety miles, but it took five days to make the journey up the Ogun River by canoe because of the strong current. Campbell observed that the main road between Abeokuta and Lagos needed to be straightened and widened, and that additional roads needed to be built from various towns to the Ogun River. There were also abundant timber resources in the area, and it only required "a small saw and shingle mill" to develop a lumber industry there.[8] Thus, Campbell believed that the portion of Yorubaland which lay between Lagos and Abeokuta was eminently suited from emigrationists because of its economic possibilities. When he reached Abeokuta Campbell stayed at Rev. Crowther's home, *Orange Cottage*, until Delany arrived.

Delany began his journey to Africa from New York on 24 May 1859 on board the *Mendi*, and reached Monrovia 12 July. The day he arrived, Delany wrote the American consul in Liberia, Rev. John Seys, to see if he could arrange a meeting between himself and President Stephen A. Benson. The president could not comply immediately with the request because of urgent business in the "leeward counties," but he did have a brief conversation with Delany before he left. They spoke with each other long enough for the Liberian executive to form an opinion of Delany and his movement. According to President Benson, Delany wanted the Liberian government to provide the financial backing for his mission to Yorubaland, but the government was not able financially to support the American's scheme. In a letter to R. R. Gurley sometime later, Benson implied that he would have supplied Delany with men and money if the American Colonization Society had been willing to increase its contributions to Liberia for a few years to offset Monrovia's support of the Niger Valley Exploring Party. Since Gurley could not promise him additional funds, Benson contended he was in no position to make any commitment to Delany. Nevertheless, the Liberian president felt that Delany's Yorubaland scheme was sound. Benson hitherto had expressed his concern over European hegemony in various parts of West Africa. He felt that Delany's movement presented exiled black men with an opportunity to extend their influence to another part of West Africa and thwart European efforts to dominate the entire region.[9]

Given Delany's criticism of Liberia since the 1840s, his effort to seek assistance from its government in 1859 requires some consideration. Most of all, he disliked Liberia's great reliance on white American philanthropy for its existence. Delany did not view Liberia as a bona fide black republic—as he did Haiti—because of the extensive influence of the American Colonization Society on its administrators. He believed Monrovia would have to sever its ties with this organization before the nation could qualify as an independent state. Even during the heyday of emigrationism in the 1850s, Delany had declared that his movement would not support those who wanted to emigrate to Liberia. Despite these earlier bold pronouncements and after many sobering and disappointing moments for his back-to-Africa scheme, by 1859 the leader of the Niger Valley Exploring Party was in no position to refuse whatever assistance he could obtain from a country he once impugned. While he was in Monrovia a group of nine citizens, Edward Wilmot Blyden among them, reminded Delany of his earlier position on Liberia; they nevertheless welcomed him to their country and asked him to make some public speeches in the city before he visited other parts of the country. Delany willingly accepted their invitation, and told them he had criticized Liberia because of his concern for the unity of the race. Hence, Delany's request for aid from Liberia was a challenge to that African government to join him in an independent course of action taken jointly by black men from both sides of the Atlantic. His intentions were reflected in the speeches he made in Liberia.

The main theme in Delany's Liberian addresses was the "Political Destiny of the African Race." In them he referred constantly to the need for unity between black men from the New World and Africa. In reporting one of these speeches, Blyden remarked that Delany emphasized unity to his audience by paraphrasing a Biblical passage from the Book of Ruth. He said, "your people shall be my people, your God shall be my God, yea, more, sir, *your country* shall be *my country*."[10] Even former president J. J. Roberts reacted to the plea for unity in Delany's speeches. Roberts believed Delany's goal of purposeful interaction between Africans and New-World blacks could be realized in Liberia. He claimed Liberians felt they were one with Delany. Although Roberts did not register a discordant note about Delany's Yorubaland scheme, he had hoped the exploring party would change course and settle in Liberia, there to work for the "nucleus [of] a Colored Nationality" in West Africa.[11]

Blyden also recorded his impressions of Delany's plea for unity. While listening to this black American speak in Monrovia, Blyden recalled that Delany always had focused his attention on Africa; and he concluded that regardless of the difficulties he faced, Delany never had faltered in his convictions or compromised his principles about Africa. Blyden knew that Delany was an avid advocate of the regeneration of Africa; that he believed its greatness would be assured if black leaders from both sides of the Atlantic worked together to make it a reality. Delany had conveyed this point of view to audiences in Monrovia. He told them that the struggle of the black race was an evolutionary one which began with the activities of the black abolitionists in America, but its logical consummation was African nationalism.[12] Throughout his stay in Liberia, Delany constantly reminded Americo-Liberians of their obligation to work for the fulfillment of a genuine union between New-World blacks and Africans. And he urged them to develop closer ties between themselves and the indigenous people.

During the thirty-nine days he stayed in Liberia, Delany traveled some seven hundred miles, visiting all of the settlements in the country except Careysburg. Because of what he had seen on this extensive tour, he made many candid statements about Liberia's potential. He seemed to feel that the people could have accomplished more and that among the elite there were too many clergymen who were serving in key administrative positions. To remedy this problem, Delany felt that Liberia needed quickly to train persons to take over from the clergymen.[13] At the time, however, Delany was encouraged when he saw that clergymen were the prime-movers in establishing Liberia's schools and its newspapers—in publication at the time were the *Liberia Herald*, the *Star of Liberia*, and the *Christian Advocate*.

Delany also expressed his views about economic developments in

Liberia. Near the St. Paul's River he saw Liberians growing rice, pepper, arrowroot, sugar cane, ginger, and coffee. However, coffee growers needed to improve their hulling and drying processes before they could produce good quality coffee. During his travels he marveled at the variety of domestic animals Liberians had, but he only saw one horse. Ignorant of West Africa's ecological problems, he admonished Liberians to cultivate large farms on which they could grow fodder for horses, and to build barns to protect their animals from the heat. With the use of horses as draft animals, Liberians would be able to increase their agricultural output. Aside from such shortcomings the economic potential of the country was evident. Along the coast Europeans owned the trading posts, but they employed black agents. In Monrovia, on the other hand, Delany saw three white merchants, two Germans, and one American; the rest were Liberians.

The head of the Niger Valley Exploring Party reserved his main criticism for the Liberian elite. He was pleased to see many private buildings constructed with bricks; warehouses made of stone, and even well-built frame houses. However, he contended that some Liberians' style of living tended toward extravagance. Such munificence sharply contrasted with the sorry state of governmental affairs and facilities in the country. In Monrovia there were few public buildings, a lack of proper harbor facilities, and a paucity of "respectable architectural designs." Except for a three and one-half mile road from Harper, Cape Palmas, to a point beyond Mount Vaughan, Delany saw no other public roads in Liberia, nor did he see paved streets in any of the towns. He urged Liberians to be more self-reliant and creative in developing their young nation. Despite his candid appraisal of the new West African state, Delany had high praise for former president Roberts and incumbent president Benson; both had monumental tasks to perform. Since the former had established the Liberian "Nationality," it was the latter's responsibility to develop the resources of the country. If Liberians were disturbed by his views, Delany claimed it was not his purpose to degrade their efforts but to remind them that they had a crucial role to play in the development of a respectable black nationality.[14] After his careful examination of conditions in Liberia, and with little more than moral support for his movement, Delany continued his journey to Lagos.

When he arrived at Lagos on 20 September 1859, he was impressed immediately with its economic potential. The town then consisted of an island six miles in circumference, with an estimated population of 30,000. Of this number approximately 1500 were repatriates from Brazil and Cuba and 25 were Europeans.[15] Lagos was the main coastal port for Yorubaland and palm oil was its chief export. Delany was elated to see that many of the merchants at the time were black men, as in Monrovia. If Lagos's economic potential appeared encouraging for Afro-American settlement, its political climate was less than tranquil when Delany arrived there. The local ruler, King Docemo, favored Delany's effort to bring Afro-Americans to Yorubaland, and told Campbell that the emigrants could settle in Lagos. Furthermore, as evidence of his support, Docemo pledged Delany a 330-square-foot tract of land as a gift.[16] But it is doubtful whether the king could have kept his promise because he sat on a very shaky throne.

Docemo had become monarch mainly by English fiat. British Consul Campbell had deposed King Kosoko because of his opposition to a strong British presence at Lagos and his apparent participation in the slave trade. Followers of Kosoko did not appreciate European interference in the internal affairs of Lagos, and their antagonism prompted the British to station a warship at the port to guarantee that Docemo remained in power. Because of the ensuing tensions between the English and most Africans, Docemo's gift of land to Delany might have embroiled the latter in the politics of its people. Perhaps such a development was averted when Delany and Campbell focused their attention on Abeokuta. As Delany did not discuss the political conditions of Lagos in his writings, one can conclude that he decided not to become involved in the internal affairs of his hosts. Delany left this coastal town on the thirtieth of October 1859, by way of the Ogun River, and reached Abeokuta on the fifth of November.

In Abeokuta Delany was reunited with his partner, Robert Campbell, who had been waiting there for him since mid-September. Chief Atambala publically welcomed both men to the community during a religious festival on 11 November. Abeokuta was an appropriate focal point for Delany's back-to-Africa movement. Like Chatham, Ontario, it had become a refuge for many black men who had escaped from slavery. In Chatham one of the leading families, the Shadds, had proved to be staunch supporters of his emigration movement. Similarly, in Abeokuta, the Crowther family became the most active advocates of Delany's African emigration scheme. The Crowthers believed that new settlers from America would contribute to Abeokuta's growth as a vital economic center in Yorubaland.

During the time that Delany and Campbell resided in Abeokuta, they encouraged Samuel Crowther, Jr., and his compatriots to form various organizations that would improve the economic potential of the town. The first was the *Abeokuta Road-Improving Society*, started in September 1859. This body planned to build five bridges and to improve the roads between Ake and the Ogun ports of Aro and Agbamaya.[17] Each member of the society contributed five bags of cowry shells (a medium of exchange in many areas of West Africa in precolonial times) to the project, and sought additional funds from English sources. Lord John Russell complied with their request by advising Consul Brand to donate $2.10 to the project.[18] The other organization formed was the *Abeokuta Lyceum*. It initiated a lecture series through which local leaders presented their views to people in Abeokuta. On 11 January 1860, Robert Campbell delivered the first talk on the topic "The Dignity of Labour,"[19] but no copy of this speech has been found. However, judging from the exploring party's good reception in Abeokuta, Campbell must have impressed those who heard his lecture. The two commissioners also met with African cotton traders at the home of Chief Ogunbonna to discuss the desirability of increased cotton production. Another dimension was added to their activities when the resident African minister for the Wesleyan Missionary Society, Edward Bickersteth, asked Delany to be the chairman for a fund-raising drive at the Wesleyan Chapel. Through these varied activities, Delany and Campbell endeared themselves to the people and the local authorities of Abeokuta. As evidence of the commissioners' impact in Abeokuta, Samuel Crowther, Jr., told Henry Venn:

> Abeokuta I can assure you dear Sir is rising fast, we can soon be ahead of Sierra Leone. Messrs. Robert Campbell and Dr. Delany are of eminent good to the country. We had the will for improvement in us lying dormant but we were aroused since their arrival, and being well informed and clever Americans, intelligent and moral men, we have done more for Abeokuta since their arrival in the space of three months than has been done in three years.[20]

This strong feeling of comradeship between the commissioners of the Niger Valley Exploring Party and people of Abeokuta opened the way for negotiations with the Alake (the highest political leader in the town) to procure a written agreement which set forth the conditions for the settlement of New-World blacks among the Egba people. The document reflected the common interest that both sides had in Delany's emigration scheme. In Article 1 the Egba authorities officially sanctioned Afro-American settlement in their communities. Articles 2 and 4 dealt with potential legal problems between emigrants and local peoples. In the first instance, if emigrants had difficulties among themselves, they would be permitted to settle them according to their own customs. If there were conflicts between emigrants and local people, however, an equal number of representatives from both sides would be selected for mediation. On the other hand, all Egba laws had to be respected by the emigrants. While both sides demonstrated a mutual respect for each other's customs through Articles 2 and 4, Egba laws would remain paramount. By Article 3, and as evidence of the sincerity of his intentions, Delany undertook only to recruit skilled persons for Yorubaland (see Appendix B for a copy of the treaty). The Alake approved the agreement 27 December 1859. The following night the Council of Chiefs and Elders of Abeokuta met at the Alake's home in Ake where they discussed the agreement and ratified it unanimously. According to Delany, the council deliberated until midnight, and Chief Ogunbonna was so elated over the outcome that he rode directly to the home of the Crowthers to tell them the good news.[21]

Convinced that they had accomplished the supreme task of their mission by having the African authorities at Abeokuta approve of their project, Delany and Campbell visited other towns in Yorubaland. In their travels northward they visited Ijaye, Oyo, Ogbomoso, and Ilorin. The two commissioners wanted to go to Rabba, but Rev. Crowther disapproved. Rabba was a Muslim town north of Ilorin, near the Niger River. The CMS wanted to establish a station there to expand its mission work into Hausaland. Crowther visited the town while on the British Niger Expedition of 1857, purchased property for the society, and left an African agent, Abegga, in charge of it. By 1859, however, the station was closed because of Muslim hostility to Christian activity in Rabba.[22] Aware of this opposition, Crowther advised Delany and Campbell not to go to Rabba. Thus the Niger Valley Exploring Party never saw the mighty Niger.

The good will exhibited toward the commissioners by townspeople beyond Abeokuta delighted them, and it helped economically too. They were always short of funds, but their financial problems for the journey northward was solved when some of the African rulers personally welcomed Delany and Campbell as brothers. At Ilorin the king gave both of them cowries for their expenses and provided them with an escort; similar hospitality was conferred on the Niger Valley Exploring Party by the King of Oyo. Delany and Campbell also were received well by American missionaries of the Southern Baptist Convention. Generally, they approved of Delany's efforts to bring Afro-Americans to Yorubaland. In referring to the activities of the "two colored gentlemen from the North now here exploring the country"

R. H. Stone said approvingly, "they declined the aid of the English entirely and acted in conjunction with influential colored and enlightened men of Abeokuta which aim I think is a very wise one."[23] The American missionaries also were impressed with Delany's medical skills. In Abeokuta he thoroughly examined the missionary, R. A. Reid, and discovered that he had a diseased heart, and Delany advised him to return to America. Reid subsequently consulted an English doctor in Lagos, who confirmed Delany's diagnosis. Thus Reid concluded that the black doctor was "a very intelligent man and seems to have good medical information."[24] Had Delany made Ogbomoso rather than Abeokuta the focal point for his movement, he would have had some missionary support for his project. Ogbomoso was the main center for the work of the Southern Baptist Convention Missionary Society in Yorubaland.

Although the commissioners greatly appreciated their good reception by Africans and some missionaries, they did not lose sight of their primary purpose, which was to explore as much of Yorubaland as possible. Always conscious of their goal, Delany and Campbell collected data not only on the geography of the areas in which they traveled but also on the political, economic, and social life of the Yoruba people. They were interested particularly in the economic potential of the towns beyond Abeokuta. Ilorin and Ibadan were two of the larger Yoruba centers they saw, but the largest market center—covering an area of twenty acres—was in Ijaye, another major town. Delany calculated that on an average day approximately five thousand people appeared there whereas on the three major market days the throngs increased to as many as twelve or even twenty thousand persons.[25] In Ilorin he saw five market centers, but the largest one covered an area of only ten acres. To Delany these well-organized and efficiently managed markets were a tribute to African industry.

Having read several European accounts of agricultural products in Africa, Delany carefully observed Yoruba farming to see if these estimates were correct. In the production of palm oil for instance, western traders claimed that Africans often lost much of the oil by bruising the kernels with stones. As far as Yorubaland was concerned, Delany felt this conclusion was faulty because the Yoruba carefully boiled and pressed the kernels. While he saw a variety of crops in Yorubaland, the care and attention employed in the cultivation of palm trees impressed him most. He was also intrigued by the way craftsmen worked to fashion metal farm implements, artifacts, weapons, and pottery.[26] These activities assured him that the Yorubas had a dynamic culture of which black men in America could be proud.

Just as he was elated over the economic potential of the Yoruba people, and took pride in their art forms, Delany also appreciated their political and social institutions. He noted that the Yoruba king had great authority in political and judicial matters, but was checked by a council of elders. Concerning religion, Delany claimed that missionaries gained Yoruba converts because the people already had a monothestic concept of a supreme being. Socially, the black American leader was happy to see strong family ties, but he argued that some parents indulged their children too much. Even on the matter of human servitude Delany maintained a pro-African viewpoint. He believed the term slave was applied incorrectly to social relations between Africans. He referred to Yoruba servitude as a patriarchial system because the outsiders were allowed to fill roles similar to the primary members of the family who "adopted" them. In Delany's opinion, such accommodation sharply contrasted with the system of industrial, gang slavery in the Western Hemisphere. But his associate had a different view. Although some forms of African slavery were not as vicious as the European variety in the New World, Campbell despised it, and vowed to work for its abolition too.[27] In Yorubaland Delany found certain exceptions to the rule of benign African slavery. In Ilorin he saw slavery similar to the European variety practiced by African moslems. He also spoke in derogatory terms about the rulers of Dahomey and Ashanti, whom he considered to be guilty of selling Africans to Europeans on the coast. Delany, nevertheless, had observed enough positive elements to conclude that Yorubaland was an appropriate place for Afro-American emigration.

On their return journey from Ilorin to Abeokuta, the commissioners of the Niger Valley Exploring Party were forced to take different routes from Oyo because preliminary skirmishes in the Ijaye War (1806-1865) had begun. After the breakup of the Old Oyo Empire at the beginning of the nineteenth century, no Alafin (Yoruba King) emerged who was able to reunite the Yoruba people. In the late 1850s, Are, the ruler of Ijaye, challenged the authority of the newly crowned king of Oyo, Adelu, but Ibadan supported the new monarch. When Delany and Campbell began their journey beyond Abeokuta on 16 January 1860, Ijaye and Ibadan forces already had clashed in two small Yoruba towns, Shaki and Okeho. By February the roads between Abeokuta, Ijaye, and Oyo were watched carefully by Ibadan soldiers, and travelers had to proceed with caution.[28] While they were not hindered on their journey northward to Ilorin, when Campbell and Delany returned to Oyo carriers refused to go further south with them. Meanwhile they were running short of funds; hence they decided to take separate routes back to Abeokuta. Campbell traveled westward to Isehin and then to Awaye. Between Awaye and Bolorunpelu he and other travelers were detained by Ibadan soldiers momentarily before they were allowed to proceed to Abeokuta. Delany took a southeastern route. King Adelu provided him with a military escort, which allowed him to pass safely through the war zone between Oyo and Ibadan.[29] While the commissioners had enjoyed the hospitality of avowed enemies in the Ijaye War, Are and Adelu, they judiciously avoided being embroiled in Yoruba politics. Both men returned to Abeokuta by the end of February, but much of the artifacts they collected had to be left at Ijaye and other towns they visited because of the war and limited funds.

Because of their financial dilemma, Delany and Campbell decided to end their stay in Yorubaland in early April and visit England before returning to the United States. Before they left Abeokuta, however, a prosperous woman trader, Madam Tinubu, asked Delany to remain in Africa and manage her business affairs.[30] At first Tinubu traded in Lagos, but in 1856 she was expelled by the British consul, Benjamin Campbell. She moved to Abeokuta and continued to have a successful business. Tinubu asked Delany to help her because she feared European economic encroachment and exploitation. She thought that a New-World black leader familiar with European economic practices could be an asset to Africans in their dealings with European traders. No doubt Delany was tempted to accept Madam Tinubu's offer, but he was more anxious to return to the United States to complete arrangements for his back-to-Africa movement. The two commissioners left Abeokuta on 5 April and reached Lagos two days later.

Delany and Campbell departed from Lagos 10 April 1860; their mission to Yorubaland appeared to have been successful. The son-in-law of Rev. Crowther, Rev. R. B. Macaulay, told Henry Venn that "these gentlemen having succeeded well in the object of their negotiations, are now returning home to wind up before they return finally to settle in this country, with their families and people." In a dispatch, British Consul Brand conveyed the same opinion to Secretary of Foreign Affairs Lord John Russell.[31] Delany and Campbell reached Liverpool 12 May 1860, where they contacted members of the Manchester Cotton Supply Association and the African Aid Society (AAS), both Delany supporters. Once the two commissioners of the Niger Valley Exploring Party arrived in England, their roles were reversed. Instead of Campbell remaining in England for an extended period as before, it was Delany who toured parts of England and Scotland to acquaint cotton merchants and other interested parties with the data obtained in Yorubaland. Meanwhile, Campbell busied himself by writing a monograph on Yorubaland, which was published in late 1860 and widely circulated in England and Scotland, where it stirred great interest in Delany's movement.

Delany was the last of a long list of prominent Afro-American leaders to visit the British Isles before the American Civil War, and the only one who had accomplished some great feat outside the sphere of antislavery agitation. Unlike Frederick Douglass and others, Delany did not go to England primarily to seek the aid of British abolitionists. Instead, he sought to persuade various interested parties to support a movement that would have bolstered both black self-determination and British industry. Thus, his African emigration scheme had a special attraction for some mid-nineteenth-century Victorian idealists, entrepreneurs, politicians, and geographers.

Delany began his tour in London where the scientific and economic aspects of the Niger Valley Exploring Party's mission to Africa received considerable attention. At first Delany spoke to a small group of members of the African Christian Civilization Committee who met on 17 May 1860 at the home of Doctor Thomas Hodgkin; there he told them of his plans to take Afro-Americans to Africa. Members of the Royal Geographical Society present were so intrigued by the information Delany presented that they invited him to read a paper on his "discoveries in Africa" to the 14 June session of the society.[32] Because of his appearance before this prestigious organization, this black explorer's journey to Africa received the same acclaim as the reports of other explorers in West Africa. Moreover, his presentation before the society enhanced his recognition in the United Kingdom as an explorer in Africa.

After Delany's lecture, he and Campbell were invited to speak at various public and private meetings in London. The event that proved most beneficial to Delany's movement was the invitation to speak at the National Club on 27 June 1860. Here Delany and Campbell made comprehensive statements about their mission to Africa, and several interested listeners invited both men to return to the club on 6 July for further talks on Delany's African scheme. After the second visit, the men at the National Club were convinced that Delany's movement could be wedded to their own interests in West Africa. They therefore agreed to establish a new organization, the African Aid Society. Among the original members were Lord Alfred Churchill, M.P., Rev. M. Thomas, secretary of the Colonial Church and School Society, and J. Lyons MacLeod, formerly British consul at Mozambique. Delany, Campbell, and the Provisional Committee of the AAS held additional talks at the Caledonian Hotel 19 July at which time the new organization agreed to provide Delany with some money to transport black men from Canada and the United States to Yorubaland.³³

Three days before the African Aid Society pledged support to Delany's movement, Lord Henry Peter Brougham of Scotland invited the emigrationist to participate in the International Statistical Congress which met in London from the sixteenth to the twenty-first of July 1860. Brougham was an avowed abolitionist. In Parliament he had worked with William Wilberforce for the enactment of the Emancipation Act of 1833. Five years later, in the House of Lords, he precipitated the debate for the abrogation of the ignominious apprenticeship system, which would end all pretexts to slavery in the British West Indies. However, it was not Parliament but the colonial legislatures that abolished the system.³⁴ After the end of slavery in the British Empire, Brougham joined the abolitionist crusade to stop slavery in other nations. Lord Brougham claimed he invited the black explorer to attend the congress because he "was a Negro gentleman of great respectability and talents."³⁵ But it cannot be denied that he had an ulterior motive for introducing Delany to this international group of scientists: Delany was living proof of the heights blacks could reach as free men.

When Lord Brougham acknowledged Delany's presence at the congress it prompted one of the American delegates, Judge A. B. Longstreet of Georgia, to walk out. He viewed Delany's presence as an affront to America, and as a hypocritical English attempt to interfere in its internal affairs.³⁶ Longstreet felt that the Delany affair was tantamount to an external "threat" to the institution of slavery in America, but Frederick Douglass, agreeing with Brougham, tended to go to the other extreme when he wrote about Delany's presence at the International Statistical Congress. He said, "Never was there a more telling rebuke administered to the pride, prejudice, and hypocrisy of a nation."³⁷ Delany felt that the matter was settled to his own satisfaction when he responded to Brougham's introduction by telling the congress he was merely a man in the presence of other men. Perhaps Longstreet's and Douglass's reactions to the incident in London were revelations of the extreme emotionalism generated among Americans over the sectional crisis. While the event was not significant in the life of Delany or Lord Brougham, it did bring some notoriety to both men in London and the United States.

Delany viewed his presence at the fourth International Statistical Congress as a significant event in his medical career and further evidence of the regeneration of his race. As an official delegate, he sat with the Sanitary Section, which was particularly concerned about ways in which pollution produced ill health. The discussions were focused on industrial centers in Europe and the United States where epidemics had become frequent. Delany told the section of his medical experiences in treating patients during the 1854 cholera epidemic in Pittsburgh. Certainly he reported nothing that could have been construed as a scientific breakthrough, but he welcomed the opportunity to discuss medical problems with knowledgeable men. He concluded, "It has been one of the greatest desires of my heart to get to London, and have advantages such as I am now enjoying."[38] Before the congress adjourned, Delany expressed his gratitude to his hosts by referring to the irony that brought him there. He was not a delegate because of his medical skills, but because some delegates sympathized with the African race; nevertheless, his presence among them was a sign of its renaissance.

Because of their good reception in London and the extensive contacts Delany and Campbell made, it became possible for Delany to make public appeals in Scotland for further support of his movement. Lord Brougham invited Delany to attend the fourth annual meeting of the National Association for Promoting Social Science, which met in Glasgow 24 September 1860, but he spent most of his time there making public speeches about his observations of Africa and its people. Simultaneously, William King and William Howard Day were in Scotland, seeking financial support for the Buxton settlement in Western Ontario. Although Day was the president of the Chatham emigration convention that sent Delany to Africa, Delany's contact with both men was minimal. Although he associated with them occasionally, he insisted on the independent nature of his mission.

In Scotland Delany captured the attention of his audiences by making them aware of the economic benefits English manufacturers could realize from supporting his movement. He convinced them that Afro-Americans and Africans working together could supply the British with large quantities of cotton, making them more independent of supplies from the United States. On the other hand, Delany appealed to the antislavery sentiment prevalent in Glasgow. He argued that if the Scots supported his movement, they would help to bring about the collapse of the economy of the American South within ten years and end slavery in the United States.[39] Despite the economic and humanitarian emphasis in his lectures, Delany made it clear that black men were not interested in white charity. He promised that any investment in his movement would realize a return. Any money procured would be considered loans that emigrants would repay after they had settled in Yorubaland. He contended that Afro-Americans, even in the northern states, were not able to realize their potential because of discrimination, but in Africa they would rise to a status equal with white men. Thus, his objective was not charity but sufficient funds to get the project started in Africa.

Delany impressed his listeners in Glasgow because he provided them with primary information which helped to correct the usual distorted views of West Africa. A reporter who heard the black explorer speak made this comment:

> His lecture gave a more vivid idea of Africa and its people than can be had from all the geographical and topographical works we have read. It was a sketch from nature, and devoid of those exaggerations and modifications which are considered necessary to satisfy the preconceived and conventional rules of art. . . . These lectures will be highly useful in correcting the false impressions which prevail in this country about that vast, and but superficially explored quarter of the globe.[40]

Most of all, however, his audiences were pleased to hear of the potential for large-scale cotton production in Yorubaland.

Delany's Glasgow audiences, like those in London, saw his journey in Africa as a worthy achievement. They believed his exploration in Yorubaland was as significant as David Livingstone's work in Central Africa.[41] In several newspaper accounts of his lectures, Delany was referred to as "another African traveller" whose work complemented Livingstone's view about the great industrial resources of Africa. Delany's movement, therefore, deserved Scottish support through the African Aid Society and the Manchester Cotton Supply Association. As a result of his determination and the conviction with which he spoke, Delany was able to persuade some Glasgow merchants to sign agreements to purchase cotton from Yorubaland. He promised to supply a Glasgow firm, Crum, Graham and Company, and other merchants with cotton and other agricultural products that would be grown by emigrants in Yorubaland.

Besides making people in Glasgow aware of the economic potential of Yorubaland, Delany frequently alluded to the view that Africa would be the locus for the regeneration of the black race. It was evident that this pan-African ideal was strengthened by his experiences on the mother continent. Being there and working with Africans had a greater impact on the lives of Delany and Campbell than all the books they had read about their original homeland. In Yoruba country both men claimed that they sensed a feeling of solidarity because they were identified with the people "in race and descent." As a result of this bond with Africans, Delany and Campbell vowed that their only goal in life was to settle in Africa.[42] To his audiences in Glasgow Delany stated his position more poignantly when he said, "he had never been able to look upon America as his home, but rather felt as if he had been born in the wrong place."[43] His affection for Africa was so strong, and he spoke with such passion on the subject, that he left the citizens of Glasgow with the impression that the greatest achievements of black men would not be realized by those living in America or the West Indies but in Africa.

Assured of support in England and Scotland, the Niger Valley Exploring Party ended its journey as it had begun: Delany and Campbell returned to America separately, but triumphantly, despite chronic financial difficulties. While people in the British Isles were more concerned about the economic aspects of the journey, in America black men recognized it as an accomplishment in itself. It provided them with an inside view of Africa and its potential.[44] Moreover, when Delany left for Africa he had been on trial among black leaders in America. When he started his emigration movement in 1852 they—Frederick Douglass in particular—did not believe he was serious. After his return, many became convinced that he was sincere about achieving his pan-African goal. Delany left Liverpool 13 December 1860 and arrived in Chatham, Ontario, 29 December, forty-five days before the Civil War began. No doubt at that moment Delany could not foresee that political conflicts on two continents would contribute to the failure of his back-to-Africa scheme. Instead of the Niger Valley Exploring Party being the initial step in a new effort at Afro-American–African cooperation, the journey to Yorubaland proved to be the only bright spot for a movement that faced insurmountable odds from beginning to end. However, their travels in Yorubaland proved to be a unique achievement in a field that was supposedly reserved for Europeans.

6

The African Dream Deferred

When Delany and Campbell returned to North America in 1860 they were confident that the plan to take emigrants to Yorubaland would succeed. However, forces were at work in America and Africa in 1861 and 1862 which prevented Delany from realizing his pan-African dream. During these years, emigration organizations had multiplied and they urged free blacks to migrate to Yorubaland, Haiti, Jamaica, or Liberia. Ironically, this pressure on Afro-Americans and black Canadians to leave the continent came at the very moment when the Civil War presented them with the opportunity to participate in the struggle to free millions of their brethren enslaved in the South. Hence, many of those who considered going to Africa with Delany or settling elsewhere in the black diaspora had changed their minds by 1862.

By then Delany's backers in Britain also had shifted their emphasis. Members of the Manchester Cotton Supply Association and the African Aid Society, who agreed to provide financial support for Delany's African scheme, tried to use their support as a justification for the extension of British authority and commercial activity beyond Lagos. In 1861 and 1862, however, British missionaries in Abeokuta opposed the expansionist design of Delany's English supporters and they questioned the validity of the treaty he made with the Alake in 1859.

Robert Campbell was the only one from Delany's back-to-Africa movement fortunate enough to return to Africa. While Delany was lecturing in Scotland, Campbell traveled to the United States and lectured to audiences in New York, New Jersey, and Pennsylvania. In New York he spoke to members of the American Geographical and Statistical Society about his adventures and observations in Africa. He told members of the society that he was convinced that the political and socioeconomic institutions of the Yoruba people had allowed them to build their own civilization. Campbell expressed similar views to audiences in New Jersey and Pennsylvania. However, it was in Philadelphia that he obtained support to begin the journey back to Africa, much of it from members of the Pennsylvania Colonization Society. By the summer of 1861, Campbell had raised sufficient funds to purchase a cotton gin and press to take to Africa and to pay the passage to London for him and his family.[1]

In London Campbell did not find the British government as receptive to his request for a free passage to Lagos as in 1859. Its reluctance was based on Lord John Russell's new policy toward Delany's Yorubaland scheme. He had decided that the Foreign Office would aid emigrants from Canada and the United States only after they had reached Lagos. Delany had been advised of this policy four months before Campbell applied, when he too tried to obtain free passage back to Africa.

Unable to secure help from the Foreign Office as a member of Delany's contingent, Campbell appealed to the British government as one of its subjects from the West Indies who wanted to settle permanently in Africa. Lord Russell argued that free passage for Campbell would set a bad precedent. Compliance would encourage other new world emigrants to seek aid from the government, and it would be a charge against the British exchequer. Furthermore, the Foreign Office informed Lord Alfred Churchill that the African Aid Society and the Manchester Cotton Supply Association should have paid for Campbell's return to Africa since they were the sponsors of Delany's African scheme.[2] When the government would not yield to the pressure of Delany's supporters in Britain, the latter supplied the funds for Campbell's passage back to Lagos. In addition to being the only one from Delany's movement to return to Africa, in 1863 Campbell began publication of the first English language newspaper in Lagos, the *Anglo-African.*

Delany now was the only one left from his pan-African movement. Unperturbed by this circumstance, he went on an extensive lecture tour in 1861 and 1862—primarily in the northern states—to seek new converts for his Yorubaland scheme. He spoke passionately yet authoritatively about Africa, after emphasizing what he considered to be the important reasons for emigrating there. First, if Africans and Afro-Americans grew cotton on a large scale in Yorubaland, British merchants could buy it from them instead of Americans, and this commercial realignment would contribute to the downfall of slavery in the South. Second, black men from the Americas needed to go to Africa to work with the people there to develop the natural resources of the continent. Third, the signs of the time demanded that they go to Africa to help thwart the imperialistic designs of the European powers. Since Africans were the only black men who had not been completely subjugated by whites, Delany thought that their independence and their cultural legacy had to be preserved. To assure the fulfillment of these three goals, Delany said he was willing to sacrifice himself and his family for Africa.[3] As he traveled and lectured, however, he had to compete with the representatives of other movements seeking black emigrants from the northern states and Canada.

The first clash between Delany and other emigration movements occurred early in 1861. At this time he was involved in a heated debate with his friend Rev. Holly, the chief advocate of emigration to Haiti. While Delany was in Africa, the government of Haiti appointed a white journalist, James Redpath, to be its official emigration agent in the United States. Delany could not understand why Holly had not protested such a racially denigrating action. To him it was a blatant violation of the principles of black nationalism and self-reliance adopted in 1854 at the Cleveland emigration convention. Redpath's position was another instance where a white man had been given the most prominent job in an organization designed primarily to aid Afro-Americans. Delany argued that Redpath should not have been given the position of chief agent when there were qualified Afro-Americans available because no white man was capable of determining the destiny of black people.[4]

Delany believed Redpath's appointment was proof that Holly had lost control of his own movement, and had compromised the principles of a Black Nationality. As if to show his friend the proper attitude a black leader should have, Delany referred to himself as one who was completely devoted to his movement: "My duty and destiny are in Africa, the great and glorious land of your and my ancestry. I cannot, I *will not* desert her for all things else in this world, save that of my own household, and that does not require it, as it will thereby be enhanced."[5] But Holly viewed Delany's remarks as a personal attack on himself and Redpath. In response, Holly revealed his longtime objections to the way Delany had managed his emigration convention. Holly claimed that he was more willing to work with white abolitionists who were sympathetic to Haitian emigration than with critical black leaders. Then he argued that the government of Haiti made Redpath its chief emigration agent in the United States because Delany's emigration convention had not fully supported the ideal of Haitian emigration. Moreover, Holly claimed he was more consistent than Delany in pursuing emigrationist goals. He had committed himself to Haitian emigration at the 1853 Amherstburg, Ontario, convention and he had never deviated from that position. Delany, on the other hand, was guilty of duplicity because he gave the members of his own movement the impression that he favored repatriation to Central America when he was interested only in going to Africa. In a final emotional outburst, Holly showed his disgust with Delany's attack on Haitian emigration by attributing his friend's inconsistency to some trick he must have learned from "some savage tribe in the jungles of Central Africa."[6]

Despite Holly's objections to criticism about Redpath's appointment, Delany was correct. When the government of Haiti and Redpath launched their massive drive in the fall of 1861 to woo thousands of blacks to a new existence in Haiti, Holly was not listed as one of the agents for the movement, yet he continued to urge Afro-Americans to go there. At the time, Holly published his lengthy essay, *Thoughts on Haiti*.[7] It was a discourse on his principles for emigration to that black republic. Like Delany, Holly did not believe in the establishment of an autonomous Afro-American colony, but that émigrés should integrate into society and serve Haiti unselfishly. He admitted that the country was deficient industrially, socially, and educationally and therefore shared Delany's belief in selective emigration. He proposed the training of a large corps of Afro-American youth in theology, the arts, and the sciences. After their formal education had been completed, each would head groups of twenty-five emigrants who would settle in various Haitian communities. Through such leavening, Haitian society would improve morally, scientifically, and economically. Then the country would be in a position to withstand the pressures of mass emigration. Neither the government of Haiti nor Redpath, however, was willing to adopt Holly's scheme.

At the very moment that Holly advised against mass emigration, the government of Haiti intensified its drive to lure non-whites to the republic. An invitation from President Fadbre Geffrard was published in the *Weekly Anglo-African* urging blacks and Indians to join Haitians in building a viable, self-sustaining black republic in the Western Hemisphere, thus restoring Haiti to its former prominence as "Queen of the Antilles." President Geffrard's desire to make Haiti a viable state was genuine. He was one of Haiti's most progressive leaders. Between 1859 and 1867 Geffrard built several public schools, a medical college, and initiated public works projects. He also obtained American recognition of Haiti in 1862.[8] Simultaneous with the government's invitation to black and red men in America, the Haitian Bureau of Emigration in Boston published several circulars to acquaint prospective emigrants with the conditions for emigration. Haiti promised to provide at least three acres of land to homestead, to grant civil and religious liberties, to construct communities with schools and churches at government expense, and not to conscript emigrants into the national army if they formed their own drill units.[9] Having received official permission to offer people these privileges, Redpath believed his agents would recruit at least 10,000 emigrants.

This optimism by the director of the Haitian Bureau had been reflected in early reports by Redpath's agents. Dr. J. B. Smith, agent for Pennsylvania, found that sentiments for emigration to Haiti had increased in such towns as Norristown, Reading, Darby, and Pottsville. John Brown, Jr., was able to encourage many black Canadians to move to Haiti, but not before he promised them that they would travel there in British ships. The Bureau's agent for the midwestern states, H. Ford Douglas, was not as successful as some of his colleagues. He discovered that most Afro-Americans in Wisconsin, Illinois, and Michigan were reluctant to leave their homes because they believed they would benefit from the industrial growth in the midwestern states. Thus, Douglas closed his emigration agency in Chicago.[10]

Redpath's plans to obtain emigrants were so ambitious that one of his agents, William Honeybun, was able to persuade some black families from Bermuda to resettle in Haiti. Redpath sent Honeybun to Bermuda in the summer of 1861, and three black leaders there, William R. Perinchief, David Tucker, and J. H. Thomas, agreed to work with him. Through the efforts of these men, thirty-five Bermudians, including Perinchief, left St. Georges on 15 August 1861 bound for Haiti. More did not emigrate because they were suspicious of American-based movements and fearful of being sold as slaves in the United States. To reassure those who did go, Honeybun had to arrange to send them to Haiti in a British ship that did not stop at an American port.[11]

Delany and his African scheme could not compete effectively with the Haitian emigration movement. Redpath had the backing of a government which allowed him to establish his headquarters in Boston, employ agents, and pay for the passage of emigrants. Delany, however, had no tangible support from the Egba people of Abeokuta, and the African Aid Society and the Manchester Cotton Supply Association were unwilling to make a maximum investment in an untried African scheme. However, the "success" of the Haitian emigration movement was unimpressive.

Often Redpath had to borrow money to supplement the funds he received from Haiti because of the added cost of boarding emigrants in Boston and New York before they left for Haiti. Moreover, Redpath was not able to overcome mounting black opposition to Haitian emigration. Mary Ann Shadd Carey of Chatham, Ontario, was probably the most vociferous opponent of Redpath's formidable campaign to transport hundreds of blacks from North America to Haiti. She claimed she had to raise her voice against the Haitian scheme because black and white radical abolitionists appeared to be complacent and apathetic about it. She noted that William Lloyd Garrison seemed to be silent on the issue. And for the first time in thirty years "our Pennington's, our Delany's, our Smith's and Browning's have been cuffed into silence."[12]

Mrs. Carey protested that black people in the northern states and Ontario had been overburdened with movements to take them away from the continent, and that the Haitian scheme was a dangerous white conspiracy. Like Delany, she objected to Redpath's leadership, primarily because he was not an abolitionist of long standing who had worked for the elevation of her race, and she castigated Afro-Americans whom he employed as agents. She saw them as opportunists who were more interested in the meager wages they received from Redpath than the welfare of their brothers, and they did not seem to mind the conflicts they had created in black communities. She concluded that these agents were inhumane men who selected emigrants indiscriminately and sent them to their doom in an inhospitable and unproductive country.

Mrs. Carey presented much evidence to substantiate her charges. On one occasion she had observed more than one hundred emigrants from towns in Illinois and Windsor and Buxton, Ontario, congregating in Chatham en route to New York where they would embark for Haiti. Since most were older people, without the means to support themselves, she concluded that they would not survive in Haiti. In addition to these poverty-stricken types, Redpath's agents had encouraged some black Canadian property owners to sell their farms and move to Haiti. Mrs. Carey contended that agents William Wells Brown and John Brown, Jr., were able to rally these emigrants by urging them to give up life in a cold country, where they were the victims of racial prejudice, for a more leisurely way of life in a tropical country among their own people. To counteract the activities of Redpath's agents in Western Ontario, Mrs. Carey and other black leaders held a mass meeting in Chatham to condemn emigration to Haiti. At the end of her address to this assembly, Mrs. Carey presented a series of resolutions, which embodied her protests against the Haitian emigration movement, and they were unanimously adopted by those present.[13]

Between the winter and spring of 1861, many Afro-Americans

joined black Canadian leaders in their protest against emigration to Haiti. This opposition was prompted by frequent reports of the adverse conditions the emigrants had to endure in their adopted home. An emigrant who had returned to the United States, J. W. Duffin, claimed that many Afro-Americans had difficulty in Haiti because they were inadequately led and were unfamiliar with the culture of the people. This leadership vacuum existed because highly skilled persons were scarce among the emigrants. Another returnee, Edmund B. Molson, said that the poorer class of emigrants would never be successful in Haiti because job opportunities were limited and only a few were able to find menial jobs with white residents. Isaiah Jones, a returnee from Windsor, Ontario, disliked the political and social conditions in Haiti. He felt that President Geffrard's regime was dictatorial and oppressive because it denied freedom of assembly for groups of more than fifty persons, and freedom of the press was not permitted in the country. Jones disliked Haitian culture and complained that many of the local people resented the influx of Afro-American emigrants.[14]

The protest was triggered further by reports of the death of emigrants in Haiti. Among them were Mary O. Monroe and her two sons, the wife and children of Rev. William C. Monroe of Detroit, president of Delany's emigration convention from 1854 to 1856. Because of his long residency in New Haven, Connecticut, as an Episcopalian clergyman, Holly was able to persuade nearly one hundred Afro-American residents of that city to emigrate to Haiti, but many of them died after being there less than one year. When black residents of New Haven heard of these tragedies, they held a public meeting in the African Methodist Episcopal Zion Church where they adopted resolutions condemning emigration to Haiti and labeled Holly an enemy of his race.[15] Shortly thereafter Holly's wife died in Haiti.

Since they were predominantly protestants in religious orientation, many Afro-Americans resented the Catholic influence in Haiti. In November 1861, the Catholic Church appointed one archbishop and four bishops to Haiti. The editors of the *Weekly Anglo-African* saw the nominations as an initial step to return Haiti to white rulers, just as they viewed Redpath's activities in America as part of the overall conspiracy. For permitting Catholic preeminence in the country, the editors said that Haiti's government was "the most imbecile, degrading, pretentious, that were ever set up as national defenders of a peoples rights."[16]

After reading the editorial in the *Weekly Anglo-African*, Delany decided once more to speak out on the Haitian issue. He charged that Haiti no longer had the potential to become a powerful black state. Its territory had shrunk considerably because Spain still controlled most of the island. For Delany, then, the entire island of Hispaniola was the state of Haiti. In 1804 Haiti consisted of the western end of the island, but in 1822 President Jean Pierre Boyer annexed the eastern region, Santo Domingo. When he was overthrown in 1843, the Spanish took advantage of the political conflict in the west, drove the Haitian forces out of the eastern region, and formed the Dominican Republic. Between 1847 and 1859 Haiti's emperor, Faustin I, tried to recapture the eastern region twice, but failed. The new president, Geffrard, had no expansionist designs. He confined his rule to the western region, now known as Haiti.[17] With limited territory and a rising population, Delany believed Haiti's economic problems would be compounded because its limited resources had to be shared with more people, and the influx of Afro-American emigrants only added to the problem. Furthermore, the pan-African advocate felt that Haiti's government had violated the cardinal principle of black self-determination by permitting white men to be the major religious leaders in the country. He concluded that the Catholic Church would make Haitians subjects of the hierarchy in Rome and more dependent on the French economically. Delany, therefore, urged his people to go to Africa where there were unlimited resources and territory and no population pressures.[18]

Emigration to Haiti was not the only movement with which Delany had to compete in 1861 and 1862, for blacks had also been urged to go to Jamaica. A few Afro-Americans migrated there in the early 1850s, including Rev. Henry Highland Garnet, a radical black abolitionist who became a Presbyterian clergyman in 1852 and was appointed a missionary to Jamaica. Although a devout worker among his people, a severe illness forced him to return to the United States in 1855.[19] In the early 1860s Garnet supported Delany's back-to-Africa movement but later shifted to Haitian emigration. Simultaneously, another black clergyman, Rev. William R. Newman, focused his attention on Jamaica. At first he worked among emigrants in Haiti under the auspices of the American Free Baptist Mission, but often he clashed with Haitian authorities and emigration agents. While in Haiti, many emigrants spoke to Newman about leaving the republic for resettlement in Jamaica, and their preference inspired him to return to North America to promote repatriation to Jamaica. In Chatham he found some support because many black Canadians had become disillusioned when white Canadians tried to establish separate schools for their children in Chatham and Dresden. Many blacks told Newman that if they could get a good price for their property they would go to Jamaica. Newman settled there himself in September of 1861.

Newman was as bitter about life in America as Delany. From his adoptd home in Jamaica, he urged Afro-Americans to leave the country as a rebuke to the "Christian Hypocrites" living in North America. He became so enraged over the racial conflict in the United States that he unleashed his emotions in this admonition to Afro-Americans: "Let them raise their own cotton and bread, and wear their own cloth and cook their own food. Let them fight their own battles, and pay the expenses of the war. Let no colored man so degrade himself and his race as to take up arms for any people who permit them to do so because they can't do without them."[20] Newman's appeal attracted a few black Canadians and Afro-Americans to Jamaica. Once in Jamaica, though, he and his few supporters discovered that there was little enthusiasm among Jamaican leaders and British officials for North American blacks to settle there.[21]

While various leaders were encouraging emigration to the Caribbean area, the government of Liberia decided to compete for emigrants and sent one of its most distinguished citizens, Alexander Crummell, to America to invite his brethren to yet another black republic. As he traveled in America in 1861 and 1862, he reminded Afro-Americans of their primary obligation to Africa. It was their ancestral home and they had to participate personally in its regeneration. In the spring of 1862 the Liberian government tried to make its appeal more attractive. The legislature sent two more spokesmen to the United States, Edward Wilmot Blyden and J. D. Johnson, and it offered prospective emigrants free passage to Liberia, farmland, medical aid, and support for six months. At the time, however, Afro-Americans did not respond any more enthusiastically to Liberia's appeal than they had to Delany's, Redpath's, or Newman's.

A correspondent to the *Weekly Anglo-African*, who referred to himself as "Old Zion," wrote an eloquent reply to Crummell which seemed to reflect the general opinion of Afro-Americans toward Africa. He said Afro-Americans did not feel that they had an obligation to Africa merely because it was the home of their forefathers. Moreover, they had not reached such a high stage of development in America that they could share their achievements with Africans; they were still very much a dependent class in the country. For Crummell to suggest that Afro-Americans go on a civilizing mission in Africa when their own house was not in order was tantamount to European arrogance toward Africa. "Old Zion" ended his critique of Crummell's appeal by arguing that the leader from Liberia thought mainly of the present. He, on the other hand, foresaw a future time when Afro-Americans, through the principle of the universal brotherhood of men of African descent, would contribute to the regeneration of Africa.[22]

Throughout 1861 and 1862 Delany's confidence in his own African scheme was not shaken by the proliferation of emigration movements, but the African Civilization Society was a direct threat to his interest in Yorubaland. It began in 1858, the same year Delany's emigration convention reluctantly agreed to let him go to Africa. The competing organization consisted mainly of black and white clergymen who wanted to establish a model colony of Afro-American Christians in Yorubaland; they were motivated by the missionary activities of David Livingstone and Thomas J. Bowen in Africa. The society claimed that it was time for religious black men from America to play a major role in Africa's redemption. Their objectives were

> The Evangelization and Civilization of Africa, and the descendants of African ancestors wherever dispersed. The destruction of the African Slave-trade by the introduction of lawful commerce into Africa; the promotion of the growth of cotton, and other products there, whereby, the natives may become industrious producers as well as consumers of articles of commerce; and generally, the elevation of the condition of the colored population of our own country and of other lands.[23]

Such goals indicate quite clearly that some Afro-American clergymen in the nineteenth century had embraced emigrationism.

Just as he had opposed Delany's emigration movement, Frederick Douglass also opposed the African Civilization Society. The president of the organization, Rev. Henry Highland Garnet, asked Douglass what objections he had to a society which encouraged Afro-Americans to pursue "agriculture, lawful trade, and commerce in the land of [their] forefathers." Douglass provided several reasons for his opposition. First, emigrationist aims were psychologically damaging to the black man's thrust for freedom and equality in the United States. He saw little difference between the American Colonization Society and the African Civilization Society because both of them contributed to the "narrow, bitter and persecuting idea, that Africa, not America, is the Negro's true home." Second, Douglass thought the proposition that slavery in America would be destroyed by ending the trade at its African source was false. He contended that if Afro-American leaders worked for the abolition of slavery in America, there would be no need to obtain people from Africa. Moreover, Douglass did not think that "savage chiefs" in Africa would listen to moral and economic arguments for ending the slave trade any more than "slave traders in Maryland and Virginia." Third, he was certain that wide-scale cotton production in Africa would not destroy the agricultural economy of the South because "King Cotton in America had nothing to fear from King Cotton in Africa."[21] Finally, Douglass told Garnet that societies like his served the personal aggrandizement of their creators and not the general welfare of black people, and that they exploited Afro-Americans by soliciting men and money for residences in foreign countries.

After the open debate between Douglass and Garnet, the African Civilization Society sent its white corresponding secretary, Theodore Bourne, to London to solicit aid from the British and Foreign Anti-Slavery Society for its proposed colony in Yorubaland. L. A. Chamerovzow, executive secretary of the London organization, agreed to help Bourne, but Dr. Thomas Hodgkin claimed that many Britons sympathetic to Afro-American emigration to Africa felt it was somewhat anachronistic for a white man to be representing a black movement. Their view of Bourne as an interloper hampered his efforts to obtain support in Britain for the African Civilization Society between 1859 and 1861.

Bourne's difficulties in London were compounded because he did not associate with Delany and Campbell after they returned from their historic journey to Yorubaland. This deliberate lack of communication between the representative of the society and the commissioners of the Niger Valley Exploring Party convinced antislavery proponents in London that there was a definite rivalry between the two organizations. In the fall of 1860, Dr. Hodgkin told Garnet that he needed to resolve the leadership crisis in his society and its rivalry with Delany's movement if he expected aid from his friends in London. Throughout 1861, as Dr. Hodgkin had suggested, Garnet and his society tried to overcome their differences with Delany's movement. While Garnet visited London to repair the damage Bourne had done, his society in America joined Delany's campaign to obtain men and money for the return to Yorubaland.

Although both men focused their attention on Yorubaland, their perceptions of Africa differed. While in Britain, Delany frequently extolled African culture and traditions. But during his visit to England in 1861, Garnet seemed to be more accommodating to the European view of Africa. He emphasized the primitiveness of Africans and the necessity for their conversion to Christian ideals. Delany also appeared to be more devoted to a pan-African goal; he always claimed that his main purpose was to live in Africa permanently. On the other hand, Garnet seemed to support many black movements. In 1861 his slogan was "Immediate, Unconditional and Universal Emancipation; African Civilization; Haytian [sic] Emigration; God and Negro Nationality."²⁵ Their respective positions on the annexation of Lagos in 1861 clearly showed the ideological contrasts between them. In a speech to Birmingham merchants 15 October 1861, Garnet expressed his approval of British action in Lagos. He saw it partly as a humanitarian act that would extend Christianity in Africa and accelerate legitimate trade along the coast. When Delany heard about the cession of Lagos, however, he was infuriated and grew more determined to return to Yorubaland.²⁶

Many Afro-Americans did not agree with Garnet's approval of the cession of Lagos, and one objector felt that his endorsement was treasonable. Others directed their remarks to the British and not to Garnet. One correspondent to the *Weekly Anglo-African* asserted that the Lagos affair shook Afro-American "confidence in British sincerity for their elevation." The editors of the newspaper accused British officials in Lagos of using treachery and deceit in their negotiations with King Docemo to gain control of another strategic portion of the West African coast.²⁷ By the beginning of 1862, resentment among informed Afro-Americans had reached such a pitch that it was suggested that black leaders needed to publish a declaration opposing the annexation of Lagos to let Europeans and white Americans know that "neither the paw of the British Lion nor the clutches of the American Eagle shall hold [black men] as prey any more."²⁸

Despite ideological differences, Delany aligned himself with Garnet's African Civilization Society in 1861, but not before it agreed to amend its constitution to suit his pan-African aims. Members of the society met with Delany in New York on 4 November 1861. After listening intently to his plans to return to Yorubaland, they agreed to add a supplement to their constitution in favor of Delany's pan-African goals. The first article of the supplement, therefore, contained Delany's principle of selective emigration. He wanted only skilled persons, who could contribute to the general welfare of the Yoruba people. In the second article, the society relinquished its plan to establish a colony of black immigrants in Yorubaland and adhered to Delany's pan-African aim of Afro-American integration into Yoruba society. It read, "The basis of the Society and ulterior objects in encouraging emigration shall be Self-Reliance and Self-Government, on the principle of an African Nationality, the African race being the ruling element of the nation controlling and directing their own affairs."[29] As soon as the alliance between Delany and the society was assured, he traveled to northern cities with members of the society to obtain money and men to go to Yorubaland.

Delany and the African Civilization Society managed to recruit one hundred and eighty-six persons to go to Africa. One hundred of them gathered in New York under the leadership of Garnet. Delany's contingent of eighty-six persons came from the Western Ontario communities of Chatham and Buxton. Among them were fourteen married couples and nine unmarried persons, of the latter only two were women. Two of the adults were over fifty and four of them were in their forties; there were twenty ranging between twenty and thirty-eight years of age. Among the younger ones, twenty-nine were boys and nineteen were girls. Besides being vigorous enough to meet the physical challenge of resettlement in Africa, all of the adults in Delany's Canadian contingent had specific skills. At least half of them were farmers who had some experience in growing corn, cotton, wheat, and tobacco. Two of them could make cotton machines and presses and repair them. Some had additional skills such as brickmaking, blacksmithing, and carpentry. There were also three school teachers, several dressmakers, one pharmacist, one upholsterer, and one shoemaker.[30]

Perhaps the most notable family represented in Delany's Canadian group was the Shadds, prominent citizens in Buxton and Chatham. At the time that they planned to go to Africa with Delany, Isaac D. Shadd published the *Provincial Freeman*, an outstanding black Canadian newspaper in the nineteenth century. His wife, Amelia, planned to teach in Africa. The youngest of the family to sign up with Delany was twenty year old Ada T. Shadd, also a teacher. Thus, it would appear from the roster of persons planning to go to Yorubaland with Delany that he had every intention of honoring his agreement with the Alake of Abeokuta. His entire contingent was capable of making some contribution to the community, but the group never reached its destination.

The alliance between Delany and the African Civilization Society did not last. By 1862, many of the persons in Canada who had planned to go to Yorubaland with Delany changed their minds. Many of the men returned to the United States to fight for the Union in the Civil War; some joined the black regiment organized in Detroit, Michigan, and others volunteered for the unit of black troops formed by Massachusetts. In addition to this loss, a lack of finances and support among blacks forced the African Civilization Society to abandon all hope of sending Garnet or anyone else to Yorubaland with Delany. It transferred its support to the Haitian emigration movement and subsequently worked among the freedmen in Washington.[31]

While the protest against emigration was directed mainly toward the Haitian scheme, one anonymous writer questioned the wisdom of all emigration leaders. Although Delany, Holly, and Garnet claimed that the development of a black nationality was the basis for their respective movements, this critic believed there were inherent weaknesses in their concepts. By proclaiming the need for a black nationality, all emigrationists had accepted the popular white myth that black men never had built civilizations or made any contributions to human progress. Viewed as a whole, Africa was "the oldest, the hardiest, [and] the least pregnable of all the nations of the earth."[32] Moreover, black leaders demeaned themselves by constantly soliciting aid in America and Britain, thereby conveying the idea that Afro-Americans were not self-sufficient. After a bitter comment about the treacherous Garnet, the anonymous commentator concluded that emigrationists weakened their own cause because their actions did not match their ideals for a black nationality. As far as he was concerned, their brand of nationalism would not alter the white man's attitude toward blacks as a subservient race. Such disenchantment with all emigration movements was symptomatic of the growing sentiment to hold a national council of black leaders to deal with all of the crucial issues facing them.

One black leader, Dr. James McCune Smith, believed a national council was needed to condemn emigrationism as a divisive force among Afro-Americans. Dr. Smith was a prominent physician in New York and an active abolitionist. In a lengthy reply published in the *Weekly Anglo-African,* Delany agreed that black leaders needed to meet, but for reasons much broader than the one advocated by Smith. They needed to meet because "the present state of the political affairs of the world . . . call for and imperatively demand our attention as descendants of Africa in whole or part."[33] Continuing to see the problems of his race in pan-African terms, Delany told Smith that a National Council would afford black leaders an opportunity to set aside their ideological differences and formulate a general policy which all black people might follow. Such a declaration would alert white men everywhere to the fact that black leaders in America would not passively watch the subjugation of their race throughout the world. At the time, the cession of Lagos was as much resented by Afro-Americans as white American reluctance to let them fight in the Union

Army to free the slaves in the South. To Delany, both were manifestations of a universal conspiracy against his people. If black leaders did not speak out against such issues, he declared, "the world should justly condemn us and . . . curse our names."[34] Although he approved of the call for a national council, Delany implied that he would only work with his American brothers until he and his family left for Africa where they intended to live permanently.

Delany's letter to Dr. Smith prompted other Afro-Americans to register their support for the convening of a national council. One correspondent from Troy, New York, said he discussed the idea with Frederick Douglass, Willliam Wells Brown, and William J. Watkins, all of whom approved.[35] He felt that this meeting was justified because Afro-Americans were numerous enough to form a nation within a nation, since there were more blacks in America in 1862 than the combined population of the thirteen colonies when the Declaration of Independence had been promulgated. William E. Walker of Trenton, New Jersey, supported Delany's views on the agenda for a national meeting because white Americans needed to hear more about the black man's character and his potential power.[36] Even Gerrit Smith, a white abolitionist, called for a national meeting of Afro-American leaders; he thought they might provide moral support for those national politicians who favored emancipation.[37] Despite the overwhelming endorsement for a national council in 1861, a national meeting of Afro-American leaders was not held until 1864. In the interim, successive events made black leaders more optimistic about the future. The federal government had discarded its policy of excluding Afro-Americans from the army, and Congress had enacted legislation that established precedents for Lincoln's Emancipation Proclamation and the Thirteenth and Fourteenth amendments. The Confiscation Act of 1861 permitted Union Army officers to free captured slaves. The following year Congress abolished slavery in Washington, D.C., and the War Department began to admit Afro-Americans to the army. Moreover, many concerned black men and women from the North followed the Union Army in the South to help destitute slaves who had fled to the army camps. Hence when Afro-American leaders held their convention at Syracuse, New York, in 1864, freedom for all black Americans appeared to be inevitable; the crises of 1861 had passed. For this reason, instead of addressing themselves to the plight of black people throughout the world, as Delany had suggested, the convention leaders focused their attention on ways their people could attain equality in America.

While Delany's efforts to return to Yorubaland were being thwarted in Canada and the United States, his movement was discredited in

Abeokuta. The main opposition came from white missionaries who disliked his association with Africans and the agreement he had made with the Alake.[38] Moreover, these missionaries visualized the entrance of large numbers of North American blacks into Yorubaland as a definite threat to the effectiveness of their religious work there.[39] To maintain their privileged position, the Church Missionary Society needed to destroy Delany's movement. This imperative was one of the motivations for the publication in 1859 of the first news journal in Yorubaland, the *Iwe-Irohin*. Through this medium the editor, Henry Townsend, a CMS missionary in Abeokuta, hoped "to influence the public mind" in the town on religious and political matters.[40]

Townsend's fear of Delany's movement was based on the disdain some British missionaries had for American colonization schemes in Africa. They did not believe that the resettlement of large numbers of black people from the new world was the proper way to assure Africa's redemption and regeneration. After seeing Delany and Campbell in Abeokuta, Townsend told Henry Venn, the executive secretary of the CMS, that he feared their movements; he said, "I cannot produce the causes of my present impressions . . . but I believe a second Liberia is the real object of [their] movement."[41] Venn shared Townsend's reservations; he believed that "the two races [would] not mix."[42] David Livingstone responded similarly a year later when Rev. William King of Buxton, Ontario, asked him about the feasibility of Delany's African scheme. Some of those who planned to emigrate with Delany lived in Buxton's Elgin Settlement, founded by King. Livingstone said, "Black people from North America carry the prejudice against colour wherever they go and though many are no doubt superior to this silly nonsense I would prevent their cordial intercourse with their less enlightened African brethren."[43]

Missionaries in Abeokuta instilled this "Liberia complex" in the minds of their African converts through the *Iwe-Irohin*. An article in the April 1861 issue read in part:

> The introduction of a large number of free blacks from America filled with certain notions of freedom, republicanism, and contempt for their uncivilized fellowmen, with whom at a distance they claim a relationship, but with whom they will not sit down and dwell as brethren of the same family, cannot but be attended with the greatest danger to the native governments and people. . . . If they come here because they are not recognized in the United States of America as citizens, or if they come here because they are dissatisfied with the Government of Canada,

and if when here they refuse to become citizens of this country under the native Government, they will be to the country a people separated from all others, bound by no tie, under no restraint.⁴⁴

In addition to such strong statements, missionaries told the Egbas they should not permit North American emigrants to enter Abeokuta because they would drive them from their lands and take over their communities.⁴⁵

Townsend's opposition revolved around the land issue. He felt that the Alake had ceded land to Delany and Campbell for settlement, but Samuel Crowther, Jr., claimed this was an incorrect interpretation of Article 1 of Delany's treaty. The confusion occurred because there were two versions of Delany's treaty. Article 1 of the draft agreement which Delany and Campbell circulated in Britain and the United States stated "that the King and Chiefs on their part agree to grant and assign unto the said Commissioners on behalf of the African race in America, the right and privilege of settling in common with the Egba people, on any part of the territory belonging to Abbeokuta [sic] not otherwise occupied."⁴⁶ When Rev. Crowther read the treaty to the Alake in the Yoruba language, he objected to the last part of the article, which promised settlement on land not occupied by the people of Abeokuta. Rev. Crowther and his son, Samuel, explained to Delany and Campbell that the Alake could not assign land without the approval of the Egba people. To avoid any possible conflict over the land question, the Alake, the Crowthers, and Delany agreed to make a second draft of the treaty by changing the wording of Article 1 to read "That the King and Chiefs on their part agree to grant and assign onto said Commissioners, on behalf of the African race in America, the right and privileges of farming in common with the Egba people, and of building their houses and residing in the town of Abeokuta and intermingling with the population."⁴⁷ Then the Alake gave Delany four major reasons why he wanted the Afro-American emigrants to reside in Abeokuta:

1. That they be under his immediate control.
2. That they be within the reach of his protection from the assaults of neighboring tribes.
3. That they render him all assistance in protecting Abeokuta from the Dahomians and other invaders.
4. That the inhabitants of Abeokuta might receive immediate advantage from their superior intelligence in agriculture and other arts and sciences.⁴⁸

At the time that Townsend challenged the validity of Delany's treaty, the AAS asked Samuel Crowther, Jr., to give his view of the controversy raging in Abeokuta. He told Lord Alfred Churchill that the Alake, the chiefs of Abeokuta, and he and his father had signed the treaty. A few days after Delany and Campbell left Abeokuta, however, Balagun Ogunbonna visited the home of Samuel Crowther, Jr., to tell him that Townsend was angry because no one had asked him to participate in the treaty negotiations. Then Townsend began to spread the rumor that Delany and Campbell were hostile men, and "one day the settlers would rise against the Egba and take their town from them." Samuel Crowther, Jr., assured Churchill that Townsend could not hurt Delany's movement because the Alake and chiefs were aware of his resentment toward it, and they would never "destroy a Treaty which they themselves made and signed before competent witnesses; or prevent the return of coloured American settlers."[49]

Rev. Crowther exhibited the same confidence in Delany's emigration scheme as had his son and agreed to cooperate fully with the AAS to assure its success:

> By the help of God both myself and my son Samuel will promise the African Aid Society every assistance in our power and within our influence, and will not be backward in our cooperation as far as is in the accomplishment of the object in view, the elevation of our country; and moreso as we have known Dr. Delany and Mr. Campbell personally and thus became acquainted with the objects for which they were sent out by this Society. The promise of help from the Society in any way in their power to strengthen our hands and further our views on behalf of Africa and Africans at our request, is received with gratitude.[50]

Despite the optimism of the Crowthers, however, Townsend seemed to have the advantage in 1861. As the private secretary of the Alake, he was able to influence the thoughts and actions of the Egba ruler toward the treaty.

In the spring of 1861, Consul John Foote decided to conduct his own investigation of the treaty controversy. Rev. Samuel Crowther accompanied him from Lagos to Abeokuta and interpreted the talks between the Alake and the consul. When Foote questioned the Alake about the treaty, he denied signing it.[51] In reporting his findings to the Foreign Office Foote stated that "the supposed grants to Dr. Delany and Campbell are so much waste paper.—But they the Egbas all say let the emigrants come, we will give them farms in the same way we have given farms to Sierra Leone people, but we will not have another people among us with another government."[52] Consul Foote was convinced that missionary efforts to invalidate Delany's treaty had been successful, but the people of Abeokuta nevertheless would have permitted emigrants from North America to live there. He told the Foreign Office that opposition to Delany's movement in Abeokuta developed because the AAS constantly publicized it as a colonizing venture.[53] Richard Francis Burton, the British adventurer and explorer, was the consul at Fernando Po at the time of the treaty controversy. He presented a more subjective account of the issue than Consul Foote. Burton learned of the treaty affair when he visited Abeokuta in late 1861. He wrote a highly emotional account of it in the *Cotton Supply Reporter* of 15 February 1862, which was reprinted in the *Weekly Anglo-African* on 15 March 1862. His reactions were similar to those of the missionaries. Even if the treaty was genuine, Burton was certain that Delany's scheme would have caused intense conflict in Yorubaland between Africans and Afro-Americans.

Consul Foote's judgment of the treaty crisis was more correct, especially his conclusion that Delany's scheme was viewed generally as a colonizing venture. Such an assessment was made in America. In 1861 the editors of the *Weekly Anglo-African* saw the treaty as a de facto agreement which gave Delany the right to "colonize" Abeokuta with Afro-Americans.[54] A year later, a reporter for *Douglass' Monthly* inferred that Delany planned to take emigrants to Yorubaland to settle "upon territory duly ceded to him by treaty during his stay in Abbeokuta [sic]."[55] Since Englishmen and Afro-Americans had characterized his Yorubaland scheme as a colonizing venture, Delany and Samuel Crowther, Jr., were confronted with a crucial ideological problem. Neither man could make Englishmen, Afro-Americans, or Africans understand that their intent was not colonization but the integration of black men from the New World with Africans in Yorubaland. Perhaps Delany and Crowther were at fault as much as the AAS for the way people saw the emigration scheme; they had not publicized the revised version of the treaty, and this oversight allowed their enemies in Abeokuta to use the flaw in the first draft to discredit their work.

While the debate over Delany's treaty continued, his backers in Britain decided to embark on a new course that caused further damage to his movement. The AAS and the MCSA were preparing to use his scheme as a pretext for British expansion deeper into Yorubaland. At the time, members of these organizations firmly held that their government should have used its resources to locate new supplies of cotton in West Africa. Since Delany's Yoruba scheme promised to yield more cotton, it was essential that the British Government place a consul at Abeokuta before the emigrants arrived from North America. But Foreign Secretary Lord John Russell said public funds could not be used to sponsor private enterprises of the AAS and MCSA.[56] The campaign to persuade the Foreign Office to place a consul at Abeokuta began exactly one year after Delany had made his treaty with Egba authorities. On 27 December 1860 Lord Alfred Churchill told members of the Birmingham Chamber of Commerce of his plan to send petitions to Lord Russell and Lord Palmerston to place a consul at Abeokuta, and they approved. By mid-February of the next year, the Foreign Office received the initial petition, which contained more than 370 signatures and a copy of Delany's treaty; other petitions followed from chambers of commerce throughout England and as far north as Aberdeen, Scotland. The AAS was able to rally such support because of the economic potential of Delany's movement. Businessmen in Birmingham were not interested in cotton specifically, but in the by-products of the new venture. They foresaw Africans and emigrants buying "hardware goods" on a large scale,[57] and entrepreneurs in Liverpool, Bristol, Leeds, and Sheffield also had visions of a great market in Yorubaland for their industrial products.

To keep these businessmen interested in Delany's movement and the placement of a consul at Abeokuta, Campbell's book, *A Pilgrimage to My Motherland*, was serialized in successive issues of the *Cotton Supply Reporter* from 1 December 1861 to 1 January 1862. Excerpts of it also appeared in the *Liberia Herald* along with other information about the work of the AAS. The AAS circulated a twelve-point declaration entitled "Cotton is Bread! In England" to stress the urgency for locating new cotton supplies and how Delany's movement would serve this need. Through its public campaign then, the AAS received sufficient public support to persuade the Foreign Office reluctantly to assign a government official to Abeokuta.

Lord Wodehouse, Under Secretary for Foreign Affairs, argued that the appointment of a consul to Abeokuta was premature. He objected to another British official being placed so close to Lagos because it might cause conflict instead of smoothness in the government's operations in that portion of West Africa. Wodehouse contended that the AAS and cotton merchants wanted the government to pay for an enterprise which should have been funded by them. He convinced Lord Russell that he should use caution in dealing with Delany's backers, and advised the foreign secretary to send a vice-consul to Abeokuta first. If he proved to be successful, then a consul could be appointed.[58]

When the AAS and the MCSA learned of Lord Russell's decision to appoint an agent to Abeokuta, they launched a new campaign against the Foreign Office and sent it another round of petitions. Churchill told Lord Russell it would encourage more black men from North America and the West Indies to resettle in West Africa. Moreover, the Foreign Office had a moral responsibility to help black emigrants from America and Canada because Britain had "grown rich by the blood of the slaves."[59] When this humanitarian approach did not seem to impress the foreign secretary, the AAS and the MCSA claimed that Delany's movement provided the government with an opportunity to extend its influence beyond Lagos.

Lord Wodehouse's arguments made a greater impact on the foreign secretary than those of Delany's backers. Instead of assigning a consul to Abeokuta, the Foreign Office sent Thomas C. Taylor to serve as its vice-consul in this Egba town. Before he left Britain on 24 April 1862, however, he met with members of the AAS and the MCSA who informed him of their desire to see cotton and other agricultural commodities mass-produced in Yorubaland. Taylor reached Abeokuta in June without any advance notice from the Foreign Office to the Egba authorities. This British presumption angered the Alake and the chiefs, and they promptly told the vice-consul he could not stay.

The reasons the Egba authorities gave for declaring the vice-consul *persona non grata* reflected the entangled political crisis in Yorubaland at the time. First, the Egba were not anxious to admit additional Europeans to their community. Second, they were angry with the British because the officer who was supposed to train Egba fighting men in the modern art of warfare remained in Abeokuta only a few days before he returned to Lagos, and the Egbas believed they lost to Ibadan in the town of Ishagga because the British did not give them the military support they had promised. The third reason that the Egbas refused Taylor was the crucial one. When he arrived unannounced, they suspected the British of attempting to extend their political and economic hegemony to Abeokuta. Taylor questioned the "wisdom" of the Egba authorities' refusal to accept a British official, but Townsend told Taylor it was an inopportune time to press the issue and advised him to leave Abeokuta immediately. In all, Taylor remained in Abeokuta for twenty days before returning to Lagos.

At Lagos Consul Freeman viewed Taylor's rejection as an insult to the Queen of England, but the Egba people could avoid the wrath of Her Majesty's Government if they reconsidered and accepted the vice-consul. If they persisted in their rejection of Taylor, then the British government would demand reparations for the insult.[60] Although the Foreign Secretary concurred with Freeman's strong statement to the Egba authorities, he was not willing to force the issue of the vice-consul's residency in Abeokuta. In fact, Taylor's rejection gave Lord Russell an excuse for not meeting the demand of Delany's British sponsors. The whole episode ended when the Foreign Office advised Taylor to return to Britain.

The African Aid Society's failure to have a consul placed at Abeokuta further hampered Delany's plans. The acting governor of Lagos, William McCoskry, wanted to extend British influence further into Yorubaland. Hence he favored Delany's scheme and the appointment of a consul to Abeokuta. He also assured the Foreign Office and the AAS that Delany's treaty was valid. But McCoskry was an unpopular British official in Yorubaland. Africans believed he interfered in their internal affairs, and he mainly was responsible for the annexation of Lagos. Thus it appeared to Abeokutans that Delany was directly involved with British imperialists.[61]

By 1862, however, missionary opposition to Delany's movement had diminished. Now Townsend found himself in political difficulty. Some of the younger and wealthier emigrants in Abeokuta disliked Townsend's influence with the Egba authorities and the power it gave him. These emigrants claimed he was responsible for the younger Samuel Crowther's expulsion from Abeokuta, and they accused him of being a slaveholder and a cruel man.[62] Because of these charges, the Parent Committee of the Church Missionary Society recalled Townsend to England until 1862. During his absence, the Egba authorities urged Crowther to return to Abeokuta. Townsend's zealous attempt to discredit Delany's movement and the Africans associated with it contributed to the growing opposition against white missionaries in Abeokuta. Rev. Thomas Champness, a Methodist missionary in Abeokuta, concluded that Townsend's career in Africa had been marred greatly because of the antagonism between him and Samuel Crowther, Jr.[63] However, the missionary campaign against Delany's Yorubaland scheme was successful. While some Africans favored an influx of black American emigrants, effective missionary propaganda persuaded many to fear them.[64]

By the end of 1862, the validity of Delany's treaty ceased to be a major issue in Abeokuta politics. In fact, many of the men involved in the controversy had died, and a new movement attracted the attention of the local people. Chief Ogunbonna, a supporter of Delany's movement, died 16 August 1861. Then Alake Okukenu, who had signed the treaty but later denied it, died 31 August 1862. Basorun Shomaye succeeded Okukenu, but the political organization of

Abeokuta was altered during his regency. Between 1862 and 1865 George W. Johnson emerged as the leader of the African faction who opposed missionary rule in Abeokuta. To augment political change, Johnson's group formed the Egba United Board of Management (EUBM), which reorganized the central government of Abeokuta in 1865. The EUBM gave Shomaye the title of president-general, but Johnson was the executive secretary and real head of the government. This administrative change effectively ended missionary dominance in Abeokuta politics but came too late to serve Delany's cause.

Because of the impact of missionary opposition and the political realignments in Abeokuta by 1863, the AAS abandoned Delany's Yorubaland scheme and its hope of extending British authority to Abeokuta; however, they sought other places in West Africa, outside Liberia, to which black Americans might emigrate. It focused its attention to Ambas Bay, Sierra Leone, but white American missionaries there objected. They felt that black men from North America lacked the cultural verve to civilize Africans. After this rebuke, the AAS ceased to be an advocate of Afro-American emigration to Africa.[65] From 1863 on, then, the society became a data-gathering agency for English traders seeking new cotton supplies and economic opportunities in tropical regions of the British Empire. Such information was published in its monthly newspaper, the *African Times*.

Although his support in Africa and Britain had eroded, in America Delany continued to exhibit a determination to return to Africa. The pan-African emphasis in his lectures was just as strong in the fall of 1862 as it had been the previous year. A reporter who heard Delany speak in Rochester, New York, registered his reaction this way:

> His lectures though terribly African, had nevertheless an important American bearing. Dr. Delany himself has this bearing and cannot well divest himself of it. He cannot speak or write without speaking and writing of the race to which he belongs, whether they be found in Africa or in America. He, himself is one of the very best arguments that Africa has to offer. He is the intensest embodiment of black Nationality to be met with outside the valley of the Niger.[66]

Often, however, Delany's nationalism provoked opposition to him and his plans. It irritated black and white Americans. On one occasion, in Detroit, Michigan, a white congregation refused to let Delany speak in their church because they claimed his presence at the International Statistical Congress embarrassed the American ambassador to England.

And more moderate blacks disliked his constant denunciation of white abolitionists. When Douglass condemned him for this fixation Delany said he would not desist because he was dedicated to black "self-regeneration and the redemption of Africa."[67]

By 1863, Delany was unable to fulfill his dream of settling in Africa. He could not compete effectively with the proliferation of emigration movements in America, and in Africa the Crowthers could not overcome the missionary opposition to his pan-African designs. Their reputation in Abeokuta had been impugned because their western-style progressive ideas appeared to support further European penetration into Yorubaland. Between 1860 and 1862 the Alake's political authority was challenged by some of the Sierra Leone leaders in Abeokuta who disliked the confidence he placed in Henry Townsend and other white missionaries. Worried about his own position, and trying to placate all political forces, the Alake denied the validity of the treaty with Delany. However, Abeokutans generally did not object to Afro-Americans living among them. Even if none of these events had occurred by 1863, Delany would not have succeeded. He was too dedicated to pan-African goals; his nationalism was too bold—too extreme for his own people to accept at the time. As a result, Delany's pronouncements of Africa's regeneration fell on deaf ears; most Afro-Americans had neither developed an attachment to Africa nor felt that they had any obligation to their fatherland. When his African scheme failed, Delany joined the struggle to end slavery in the South.

7

Nationalism Revisited

By the end of 1862, Delany reluctantly abandoned his plans to return to Yorubaland. Forced to remain in the United States, the pan-African advocate again pursued Afro-American nationalist goals. He began by calling for the formation of a separate black army, consisting of volunteers from Canada and the northern states. Delany suggested that some of the states could provide weapons, while abolitionists would furnish uniforms. He felt that such an army would refurbish the black military tradition in America. Afro-Americans had fought bravely in all of the nation's wars since the American Revolution, but the Civil War was different. Delany had visualized a separate black army marching south with the Union Army, striking its own blow for the freedom of the slaves. Such an army was psychologically important, Delany contended. If it won a decisive victory over Confederate forces, it would represent a significant moral victory for the race. Frederick Douglass agreed to publicize Delany's idea of a separate black force, but he noted that the North was reluctant to train and arm Afro-Americans. Douglass felt that Afro-Americans should not wait for the northern states to act, but ought to organize their own military units and arm themselves because the federal government eventually would have to use black troops.[1]

Since the federal government was reluctant to admit Afro-Americans into the Union Army during the early stages of the Civil War, northern states began to establish their own black regiments. Massachusetts led the way when, in 1863, Governor John A. Andrew formed the Fifty-Fourth Colored Regiment. He asked George L. Stearns to employ Afro-American recruiters to staff the unit, and many black abolitionists willingly accepted the job. Among them were Frederick Douglass, William Wells Brown, Charles Lenox Remond, and John Mercer Langston. At the time Delany also became a recruiter. He and a partner, John Jones, established an agency in Chicago, which obtained contracts to enlist men for Massachusetts, Rhode Island, and Connecticut.²

Delany's recruitment materials were informative, and they reflected his nationalism. One poster, "To Colored Men," was directed at volunteers for the First Regiment of Rhode Island Heavy Artillery. It contained President Lincoln's General Order No. 233 of 21 July 1863, which assured black soldiers that they would not be enslaved if captured by the enemy. Delany also printed Charles Sumner's statement about the need for Afro-American enlistees. Since blacks enjoyed the protection of the national government, the senator urged them to join in the battle against the South.³ Delany purposely printed such authoritative statements on his posters to assure recruits that they would be supported fully by the federal government in the North and South. In addition to official statements on government protection, Delany's posters attempted to instill black pride in recruits. He described how Major-General Blunt had praised the First Kansas Colored Regiment for its bravery in the Battle of Honey Springs, Arkansas, and how three companies of the Massachusetts Fourth Colored Regiment had fought bravely at James Island. More black volunteers were needed, however, because "the millions of your brethren still in bondage implore you to strike for their freedom."

Finally, the poster "To Colored Men" provided detailed information on the monetary rewards volunteers would receive if they joined the Rhode Island regiment. The state promised to pay each volunteer a bounty of $250 and $13 monthly and uniforms, while the federal government would add a bonus of $100. In addition, families would receive support during the period of enlistment, and volunteers would receive a pension for life if wounded. Besides these benefits, Delany's agency promised to pay the volunteers' train fare to Rhode Island.

The success Delany and Jones had in recruiting Afro-Americans for Rhode Island by 1863 made it possible for them to obtain a contract from Connecticut to supply men for its Twenty-Ninth Regiment of Volunteers. For Delany, the Connecticut contract was significant. He and Jones were only sub-agents for Massachusetts and Rhode Island, but they were the western recruiting agents for Connecticut. The bounty from Connecticut was $20 less than that of Rhode Island, but Delany urged Afro-Americans to join the state's regiment because it had recognized black leadership in recruiting.⁴

He viewed the Connecticut contract as another illustration of the ability of black leaders to raise a national Afro-American army. Thus, the circular he used to recruit men from the Connecticut regiment was appropriately entitled "Black National Defenders." Coincident with his recruiting for northern states, Delany wrote Secretary of War Edwin M. Stanton and suggested that the federal government form a national recruiting agency headed by black leaders. These leaders knew their people better than anyone else, and they were more capable of obtaining volunteers because of the great influence they had among their people. Delany assured Stanton that his agency was ready to begin recruitment on a national scale. Even though the secretary of war did not reply to the letter, Delany thought that his proposal for the formation of a national black army suited the social conditions in America. Since the United States had no intention of developing an integrated army, a separate black force would permit Afro-Americans to have a discrete, yet recognized military status during the war without disturbing the racial status quo.

Despite his fifty-one years of age, Delany tried to enter the Army. He wanted to enlist as a medical officer, but the War Department denied his request. Although he was rejected, Delany was determined to present his military scheme to the government. At the same time, he had become disenchanted with the recruitment system because it permitted those in charge to exploit Afro-American volunteers. Thus, he decided to go to Washington to discuss these matters personally with President Lincoln.

Before he continued his campaign to see a black force formed, Delany moved his family from Chatham, Ontario, to Wilberforce, Ohio, in 1864. It was a logical step to take. He had taken his family to Canada to protect them from the impending consequences of the Fugitive Slave Law of 1850 and to establish the headquarters for his back-to-Africa movement among emigrationist sympathizers in Chatham. By 1854, however, the Fugitive Slave Law was no longer a threat to free blacks in the North, and Delany's movement to take his countrymen to Yorubaland had failed. Furthermore, he moved to Wilberforce so that his children could attend Wilberforce University, the first institution of higher learning operated by Afro-Americans. One of Delany's sons, Alexander Dumas, upon graduation became a public school principal in Urbana, Ohio. Another son who graduated from Wilberforce University, Faustin Soulouque, taught mathematics at Lincoln University in Jefferson City, Missouri. Although he had relocated his family in the United States, Delany spent little time with them between 1864 and 1884. He was too engrossed in the pursuit of nationalist causes to settle down, yet he provided for his family during these years. The relocation of his family to Wilberforce proved fortuitous for his childern, but it resulted in a personal tragedy for Delany. He was a close friend of Bishop Daniel Alexander Payne, the president of Wilberforce University, who permitted Delany to store his private papers, memorabilia, and artifacts on Africa in a room of the university's administration building, Shorter Hall. In 1866, Shorter Hall was destroyed totally by fire, and twenty years of Delany's literary pursuits and factual materials were lost.[5]

By 1864, Delany had become more determined to see a national black army. While conversing with Dr. James McCune Smith and Frederick Douglass about the role of Afro-Americans in the Union Army, he contended that a separate black army would be able to demonstrate its own military prowess and brave deeds. Successive generations of black children proudly would learn that their forebears played a major role in ending slavery, not as tandems to whites but as distinct units of men engaged in battles with the southern exploiters of the race. Once again, Delany thought in terms of the independent action of his people to free themselves, an attitude and ideological posture that he maintained when he spoke to President Lincoln in 1865.

In Washington, Delany stayed with a former colleague, Rev. Henry Highland Garnet, who once shared his interest in Africa. Garnet, too, had been a recruiter, but on 2 March 1864 he became the minister for the Fifteenth Street Presbyterian Church in the nation's capitol. While in Washington, Garnet served as a chaplain to black troops, and in 1865 he became the first black leader to speak to Congress, when he gave the keynote address to commemorate the third anniversary of the Emancipation Proclamation.[6]

Delany told Garnet he was not in Washington to seek favors from the government, but to present his military scheme to President Lincoln. He met the president on 8 February and urged him to form a special national Afro-American army led by black officers. This elite force would march through the South, setting slaves free and issuing them weapons to fight for the Union. Then the competent veterans from this army could train a nuclear force of forty thousand blacks who would crush any further resistance from whites after the war was over. Delany assured the president that the presence of such an army would have a positive psychological effect on the bondsmen, encourage them to fight for the federal government, discourage foreign intervention in the South, and greatly shorten the duration of the war.[7]

Considering the time, Delany's military plan was bold. By the time he spoke with Lincoln, the Union Army had won many battles against the Confederacy. But Delany sought a permanent garrison of Afro-Americans in the postwar South, which would guarantee the freedom of the former slaves. He reasoned that black men had a greater proclivity to protect the rights of their brethren than white men. If Lincoln had followed Delany's plan, the predominantly white Union Army would have become a supportive force for a vanguard of black troops enforcing the Emancipation Proclamation throughout the South. The president was impressed enough to ask Delany to explain the scheme to the secretary of war. After he had spoken with the two highest government officials of the time, Delany was allowed to enter the Army with the rank of major. By admitting Delany to the Army, Lincoln and Stanton actually ended his campaign for the formation of a government-sponsored, separate, national black force. The avowed nationalist had allowed the government to place him in a position where they could control his activities for the next four years.

At fifty-three years of age, Delany became a major in the Union Army. The secretary of war had ordered Colonel C. W. Foster, Assistant Adjutant General for Volunteers, to muster Delany into the Army for three years or for the duration of the war. When Delany learned of his commission, he thanked Secretary Stanton and vowed that he would never dishonor the position the War Department had bestowed on him. The nationalist leader, now a military officer, was assigned to the Department of the South, under the command of Major General Rufus Saxton, Superintendent of Recruitment and the Organization of Colored Troops.[8] While Afro-Americans boasted that Delany was the first black major in the American Army, his career as a soldier was haphazard. He was a black officer in a segregated military system, and it was doubtful that he would be given an authoritative position through which to develop a black army. Although the War Department had appointed Delany to the Department of the South, at first he was not assigned to a specific regiment. The instructions stated that he was to be assigned to the first black regiment to be formed by General Saxton. Moreover, to make sure there was no doubt about his rank or appointment, Colonel Foster informed General Saxton that "Delany had the entire confidence of the [War] Department."

Major Martin R. Delany began his military career as a recruiter for a newly formed unit, the 104th Regiment of United States Colored Troops. He traveled in the midwestern and eastern states, urging Afro-Americans to join the new regiment. In New York, Delany found two men whom he wanted to use as scouts, but the War Department refused to employ them in that capacity. One man, Anthony Bronwell, had been a scout for a Confederate officer until he escaped to New York; the other, Charles Henry Webb, had been a drill master for a black volunteer company in Detroit. Colonel Foster informed Delany that he refused to pay the cost to transfer these men to South Carolina because neither one of them planned to become regular soldiers.[9] This failure was merely one of a series of disappointments Delany encountered in his efforts to form a distinct national black force.

Part of Delany's dilemma stemmed from the period in which he entered the Union Army. Less than two months after Delany was commissioned, President Lincoln was assassinated. Even before that fateful date (14 April), it was evident that the Civil War would end shortly. General Robert E. Lee had surrendered on 9 April, and the last Confederate force capitulated in New Orleans 26 May 1865. Hence, Delany was in the Army for only three months of the military phase of the Civil War. This reality contributed to the diminution of any hope of organizing an elite force to protect the rights of Afro-Americans throughout the South.

In the summer of 1865, Delany began the second and final phase of his career in the Union Army. He became a military aid to the Freedmen's Bureau. On 15 July 1865, the War Department relieved Delany of his duties with the 104th United States Colored Troops and ordered him to appear at the Freedmen's Bureau headquarters at Port Royal, Hilton Head, South Carolina. Since Delany already had helped many former slaves in Charleston to make the transition to freedom, General Daniel E. Sickles sent him to work with the freedmen in the Military District of Port Royal and the Sea Islands. Because of his effectiveness there, Major J. P. Roy, Acting Inspector General for the Department of the South, recommended that the major should remain with the bureau. It was Roy's recommendation and the good reports of other officers that delayed Delany's discharge from the Army. By the summer of 1866, Major Delany had become the bureau's Sub-Assistant Commissioner of the Military Reservation of Hilton Head and its Dependencies.[10]

Although Delany was a military officer for approximately three years, his nationalistic ardor had not diminished. In early May 1865, he urged Afro-American leaders in Charleston to establish their own newspaper, to inform the freedmen of their rights, and to prepare them for their new status as citizens.[11] Later in May, Delany was one of the keynote speakers at a biracial meeting at Charleston's Zion Church; the other speakers were Chief Justice Salmon P. Chase, General R. Saxton, and R. H. Tomlinson. Speaking first, General Saxton noted that black soldiers had helped to assure a military victory, and now he expected Afro-Americans to join the "battle" for their political privileges. He promised to protect the rights of the freedmen, but he wanted all Afro-Americans in South Carolina to initiate the drive for their enfranchisement. He advised them to petition the federal government for their political rights. If they took such action, he would support their cause.[12]

In his speech, R. H. Tomlinson, Superintendent for Education in South Carolina for the Freedmen's Bureau, urged the freedmen to take a different course of action than that suggested by General Saxton. He advised them to work for a "United Party" made up of freedmen and poor whites. Then the downtrodden class of both races could petition the national government for their rights and work for the reorganization of the government of South Carolina. Chief Justice Chase was the third speaker at the Zion Church meeting, and he spoke in paternalistic terms. He said it was the responsibility of the freedmen to prove that the racial pessimists were wrong. They had to demonstrate clearly that Afro-Americans were industrious, thrifty, and capable of contributing to the growth of the nation.

The emphasis of Delany's speech was significantly different from the emphasis of the other speeches. He stated that Afro-Americans had to fight for their political rights, but that racial solidarity was essential to their progress. Delany referred to the unsuccessful Denmark Vesey insurrection in Charleston in 1822 to illustrate the dangerous tendency among Afro-Americans to divide themselves along a color line. He claimed that it was a mulatto who revealed Vesey's plans to whites, and the planter class had exploited Afro-American divisiveness to prevent racial solidarity from Vesey's time on. Delany hoped, however, that mulattoes and blacks would resolve their conflict and that both would work together as a concerted force to obtain their political rights.[13]

On 23 July 1865, two months after he spoke of black solidarity in Charleston, Delany delivered a passionate, nationalistic address to some six hundred freedmen on St. Helena Island. It was evident that Delany had not given up his concept of forming a national black army. He spoke of Afro-American regiments in the Union Army as though they were an entity, and he told the freedmen that these soldiers were the ones who had fought for their emancipation; he urged the freedmen to unite with the black veterans to prevent any further exploitation of Afro-Americans. Then Delany admonished his audience to seek the advice of enlightened black leaders before they engaged in any negotiations with whites. Whites had proved to be unscrupulous and exploitative, but educated blacks could cope with them. Furthermore, it was imperative for freedmen to know that white men had not accomplished anything that they could not achieve. Delany declared that European success in the New World was a direct result of the productivity of the African continent and its peoples; Europeans purposely had suppressed Africans in the Americas because they feared the Africans' ability to rise up and challenge them.[14]

The black Major told his listeners that there was only one, inevitable course of action left for them to take: occupy the land. Possession of land would provide the economic base for their new status. If individuals could not afford to buy land, whole black communities in the South should purchase it, raise cash crops, and share the profits. Then Afro-American producers could make whites dependent on them. Furthermore, freedmen would avoid peonage if they refused to work for their former masters for thirty cents per day. "I will not have it, the Government will not have it, and the Government shall hear about it. I will tell the Government. I tell you slavery is over, and shall never return again."[15] Instead of accepting thirty cents per day, Delany told his listeners to demand one-third of all crops that they grew for their employers.

Lieutenant Edward M. Stoeber, a white officer who heard the black Major's provocative speech, recorded black and white reactions. Some of the freedmen said Delany was "the only man who ever told them the truth," and others vowed to kill their employers. Whites who heard the Major reacted with expressions of fear and concluded that another such speech would inspire insurrection. Stoeber also stated his own objections to Delany's address. He saw the nationalist advocate as a black racist who hated all whites, and who was determined to discredit the United States. Stoeber argued that the Major purposely told the former slaves that black soldiers freed them so that they would disregard the government, and he spoke of black superiority to turn them against whites. Moreover, to white men it appeared that Delany advised the freedmen to be self-reliant because he opposed the government's policy of contract labor in southern reconstruction. Finally, Stoeber believed Delany's address was designed to urge Afro-Americans to seek equality through revolution.

After the St. Helena incident, some of the white officers assigned to the Freedmen's Bureau in South Carolina saw Major Delany as a dangerous man. One of them, Lieutenant Alexander Whyte, Jr., of the 128th Colored Troops, sent excerpts of Delany's speech to his commanding officer, Major-General G. A. Gillmore, with the notation that "there was something rotten in Denmark."[16] Gillmore relayed this information to the War Department and the commissioner of the Freedmen's Bureau, informing them that Major Delany's speech was inflammatory and designed to incite violence. For these officers, then, Delany's nationalistic overtures to the former bondsmen were incendiary in an already explosive situation in South Carolina. After 23 July, white officers worked to hasten Delany's discharge from the Army, despite his efficiency as an administrator for the Freedmen's Bureau.

If his superior officers advised him to relent, Delany ignored them. Two months after the St. Helena affair he became one of the organizers of the black convention which met in Charleston during September 1865.[17] The Afro-American leaders in the state met to protest against the "black" codes white conservatives had adopted in a special session of the legislature a month earlier, and they asked the lawmakers to recognize the political rights of Afro-Americans. Also in September, Delany began to publish articles in the *New South* of Hilton Head. By December he had written seven under the title "Prospects of the Freedmen of Hilton Head." In these articles he claimed it was imperative for the freedmen to be integrated into the southern economy.

At first Delany argued that Afro-Americans had proved they were capable of adjusting to new conditions and developments. The slaves demonstrated this in the southern agricultural economy by working at various jobs assigned to them on the plantations. But as freedmen, with the proper education and training for skilled jobs, they would become self-sufficient. Delany concluded that the use of slaves in the southern struggle against the North was clear evidence of the African's adaptability as a worker and his worth to the economy of the region.

In his articles Delany also challenged the myth that black men were lazy. As slaves, they did not energetically pursue their assigned jobs because the rewards were minimal, and they were allowed no occupational freedom of choice. As free laborers, he was certain there would be a marked difference in the attitude of black workers. After the Civil War, however, Delany felt that the black work force in the South would be cut by fifty percent. Without the compulsory labor required of all members in a family, the elderly and the young children no longer would work in the fields.

With the abrogation of slavery, the southern economy needed reorganization. Delany argued that it no longer should be a restrictive system where whites owned all property and Afro-Americans were landless. Instead, the federal government needed to redistribute the conquered lands by dividing them into lots of twenty to forty acres and allowing the freedmen to purchase them. If this plan were followed, Delany contended that the freedmen would become a productive class. Their life styles would change, and they would sustain the new economy. If the freedmen were permitted to participate in the industrial growth of the South, they would become economically equal to whites.

To accomplish the goals he outlined, Delany urged the leaders in the nation to devise a Triple Alliance for the reconstruction of the South. It would require northern capital, a just redistribution of southern land, and a highly skilled black labor force. General D. E. Sickles was intrigued by this call for an alliance. In fact, Rollin maintained that the idea prompted General Sickles to retain Delany as an agent with the Freedmen's Bureau.[18] The editors of the *New South* were also impressed with Delany's views on Reconstruction, but they concluded he was clearly partial to his own race.

Delany's military career ended in 1868. By the beginning of the year the Army had begun to discharge officers assigned to the Freedmen's Bureau, but the War Department informed Delany he would be retained.[19] In the summer, however, the assistant commissioner for the Freedmen's Bureau in South Carolina, General R. K. Scott, told General O. O. Howard that Major Delany's services no longer were required at Hilton Head. Scott claimed he found no fault with Delany's work among the freedmen, but his presence was not necessary after 1 August 1868.[20] Delany thus left the Army at an appropriate moment in the history of Afro-Americans. On 20 July 1868, Congress adopted the Fourteenth Amendment which, for the first time in the nation's history, gave blacks the legal status of citizens.

Rather than returning to Wilberforce, Delany remained in Charleston where he drifted from one political appointment to another for the next decade. The nationalist advocate continued to make polemical statements about the rights of his people, but he never held an important political office in South Carolina in the Reconstruction era. Although Afro-Americans were proud of his past achievements, Delany's tendency to remain independent in Reconstruction politics kept him from attaining a key political appointment in the state. He believed that Afro-Americans should not give unswerving allegiance to the Republicans. Instead, they needed to weigh the issues and vote for politicians who might serve their interests best. This approach to Reconstruction politics eventually caused Delany to shift his support from the Republicans to the Democrats in Charleston. Thus in his eagerness to espouse black self-determination it appeared as though Delany had joined the enemies of his race.

Delany was keenly aware that Afro-Americans needed instruction to use the new political status they had gained. Hence, he wrote four tracts on national policy for the students of Wilberforce University. The first tract dealt with the responsibilities of citizenship. He admonished the students that the status of citizens involved more than the right to vote. It implied that Afro-Americans had the right to share in the political power of the national, state, and local governments. It meant that black men had to determine their own destiny and decide who would represent them politically. It was, therefore, imperative for Afro-Americans to study political science so that they would learn how to exercise their political prerogatives.[21]

The second pamphlet apprised the students of the Afro-American's civil rights. Delany compared the civil rights of Englishmen and Americans with those of Frenchmen. In the latter instance, civil and political rights were inseparable. In Britain and America, however, civil rights were distinguished from political rights, an inconsistency which often led to political inequality. In America, a man may have had the right to vote but not the privilege to hold office. Before Reconstruction black Americans could neither vote nor hold office. However, once Afro-Americans gained citizenship, they also were entitled to their civil rights. To obtain them, blacks needed to prepare themselves for the opportunities and jobs they hoped to receive. Without proper preparation, Delany charged, Afro-Americans deserved nothing.[22]

In the third tract Delany expressed his views on the Constitution of the United States. To him, the Constitution was not designed to protect the rights of the people but to regulate and determine the functions of various branches of the government. Delany was convinced that Thomas Jefferson intended the Declaration of Independence, like the Magna Carta, to be the constitution for the new nation. But the founding fathers had circumvented the Declaration of Independence to form an "ambiguous document" that did not properly guarantee the rights of all Americans.[23] Delany further stated that until the end of the Civil War the Constitution was a fraudulent document which did not apply to Afro-Americans. Thus he advised black students to study thoroughly the constitutions of France and Britain and compare them with that of the United States. This would give them an awareness of the modern principles of human rights, which could be guidelines for the attainment of equal rights for black Americans.

The last tract dealt with the status of the Confederate states. He felt that radical Reconstruction was just. He admitted that southern states that disapproved of the present federal system had the right to withdraw from the Union and establish their own government, but not on any portion of the national territory. Thus Congress acted correctly in passing legislation to reorganize the governments of the seceded states. The federal government's action was just because it validated the new political status for Afro-Americans. Whatever happened to the South was the result of its own rebelliousness.[24]

Delany expressed his political views to the students at Wilberforce because he believed that future black leaders had to be educated men. This elitist concept contrasted with his view of black masses in the South. One year after he published the Wilberforce tracts, Delany issued his observations about the activities of Afro-Americans in South Carolina. He deplored their lack of political sophistication, and felt that freedmen often were impudent. In addition, they allowed themselves to be exploited by white opportunists from the North and the South, and they had not tried hard enough to educate themselves. Delany was appalled also at the sight of armed freedmen at political rallies, and by the fact that the mulatto-black conflict was as evident in Charleston in 1871 as it had been earlier in the century. Delany concluded his remarks by accusing the Republicans of deliberately discriminating against Afro-Americans, even in the nation's capital.

After he read his "old friend's" remarks, Douglass made a candid but sympathetic reply. If Afro-Americans lacked political sophistication, it was not their fault entirely because slavery did not prepare them for freedom. Even the insolence of the freedmen was understandable. Douglass said, "The beggar suddenly raised to opulence is more offensively and insufferably insolent than the man reared and educated in wealth."[25] Being duped by carpetbaggers and scalawags also resulted from the slave background. Hence blacks were no different from the masses of workers or white poor who were used by designing men for their self-aggrandizement.

Douglass explained that Delany's disappointment was due to his impatience. The nationalist leader failed to realize that the freedmen, though many were adults, were going to school for the first time and that immediate success and sophistication was not possible. Delany needed to be more tolerant until the conditions for the freedmen had improved.

Douglass further chided Delany for objecting to black aggressiveness during Reconstruction. Freedmen were compelled to carry arms to protect themselves from their former masters. Indeed, Afro-Americans had not initiated the tradition of bearing arms; white men in the South did so long before Reconstruction began. Douglass deplored violence, but he said he would not ask his people to remain "lambs [when] . . . whites insist upon being wolves. Assault compels defense."[26] While Delany abhorred the freedmen's assertiveness, Douglass saw it as another manifestation of the black man's liberty in the South. Good manners typified the enforced submissiveness of slavery. The veteran abolitionist leader said, "it had a real significance then. It has none now."[27]

Finally, Douglass objected to Delany's accusation that Republicans deliberately discriminated against Afro-Americans. Delany wanted the Republicans to hire blacks according to their percentage of the national population. Douglass did not argue against this ideal but claimed that it was not practical at the time. The period after emancipation had been too short to expect to find enough trained black people to take one-eighth of the positions in politics, literature, and the arts. Douglass agreed that Afro-Americans had the potential for proportionate equality, but he felt that Delany should have realized that circumstances would cause inequalities between the races until Afro-Americans had achievements in all fields of endeavor.

The 1871 exchange between Delany and Douglass was crucial to an understanding of the ideological difficulties Delany encountered in South Carolina. Delany still felt that he knew the best direction his people should take. He constantly talked of an independent course of action, but southern black leaders favored an alignment with the political party that set them free. He insisted on self-determination at a time when his people were making the transition from slavery to freedom. Thus Delany's earnestness of purpose appeared contradictory in face of the general black conception of the correct course of action during Reconstruction. Douglass was aware of Delany's dilemma, admonished him in cordial tones, and hoped that both of them could continue to work together for the elevation of their race.

Ironically, Delany was a minor figure in South Carolina politics; a fact that prompted W. E. B. DuBois to omit his name from a list of prominent black leaders in the state during Reconstruction.[28] He was recognized as a champion of his people's rights, and his journey to Africa and his military rank had gained him notoriety. To honor the major, a black National Guard unit in Charleston was called the Delany Rifles.[29] However, neither blacks nor whites in South Carolina seemed anxious to elect him to high political office. Delany's nationalism was his own undoing. For this reason his political activities in the 1870s were an exercise in frustration.

Perhaps his political problems began before he was discharged from the Army. While assigned to the Freedmen's Bureau, he initiated an investigation of the Freedmen's Savings Bank, established to encourage former slaves to be thrifty. During 1865 and 1866, in Charleston alone, blacks had deposited $18,000; such frugality contradicted the stereotypic view that Afro-Americans were spendthrifts. As branches of the bank opened throughout the South, the fraudulent activities of some of the bankers increased accordingly. At first Delany reminded General Saxton that Army officers with the Freedmen's Bureau had collected $475,000 from blacks, and that the government was obligated to safeguard this money. Then he wrote to the general inspector of the bank and told him there were illegal practices at the Beaufort branch, which was under the jurisdiction of General Saxton.

After his discharge the inspector general encouraged Delany to continue his investigations, which he did at his own expense. He completed his tour of the branches by May 1870 and went directly to Washington to report his findings to General John Eaton, head of the Department of Negro Affairs. After listening to Delany's report about the fraud rampant in many branches, Eaton asked Delany to repeat his findings to the president of the bank. Delany spoke to the president, who became angry and denied that there was any corruption in the branch banks. Delany later claimed that this investigation of the Freedmen's Savings Bank marked the beginning of his political troubles in South Carolina;[30] he believed that the Republicans never forgot his role in exposing the corruption in the bank and therefore excluded him from any important appointive position during Reconstruction.

Because he had depleted his personal funds during the investigation of the bank, Delany found it necessary to seek a well-paying position in 1871. First, he failed to convince his former superior officer, General R. K. Scott, then governor of South Carolina, to appoint him to the post of jury commissioner. Second, he was unable to win appointment as the United States minister to Liberia.[32] Then in 1872 a small biracial group of Independent Republicans interested in reform, including such black leaders as Rev. Richard H. Cain and Joseph H. Rainey, tried to nominate Delany for secretary of state. In a compromise, however, to obtain the nomination of another black politician for state treasurer, Francis L. Cardozo, the Independent Republicans dropped Delany from the ticket, but he still campaigned for them.[32]

By associating with the Independent Republicans, Delany became involved in a bitter political struggle in the state. Regular Republicans were suspicious of the Independent Republican faction from Charleston. The *Beaufort Republican* accused the *News and Courier* of Charleston of falsely trying to portray Reuben Tomlinson, the Independent Republican nominee for governor, and Delany as sincere men. The Beaufort paper characterized them as opportunists who would say publicly whatever they were paid to say.[33] Moreover, the editors of the *Beaufort Republican* felt that a majority of the residents of Charleston did not respect either Delany or the *News and Courier*. They were certain that if Tomlinson were elected, he would raise the tax rates to pay for fraudulent state bonds. Delany did not therefore improve his political status in the state by supporting a dissident group of Republicans.

Rev. R. H. Cain, a black Republican leader in Charleston, persuaded Delany to break with the Independent Republicans to campaign for the regular Republican gubernatorial ticket. Delany again was disappointed, because after the election of 1872, the newly elected scalawag governor, Franklin J. Moses, Jr., did not reward many black leaders who had campaigned for him. Rev. Cain asked the governor to appoint Delany to a political office because of his dire financial condition. He reminded Moses that Delany "had staked all on *your word*,"[34] but the governor ignored Cain's plea. By the summer of 1873, a disillusioned and bitter Delany turned once again to writing. He planned to produce a comprehensive *History of the African Race in America from 1502 to 1865*, which he hoped would become a standard reference work for Afro-American history. He asked people to loan him any material pertinent to the black man's experience in the nation, a state, or local community,[35] but nothing came of this project. By 1874 Delany had thrust himself back into Reconstruction politics. He began by embarking on a personal campaign to encourage his people to chart a new political course. He was convinced that the Republicans were using Afro-Americans for their advancement in the South; therefore, he wanted them to leave Lincoln's party and join the Democrats. In a speech he made at the State House in Charleston in September of 1874, he attacked the Republicans. When Governor Moses did not appear for the meeting, Delany was asked to speak. With his usual candor, he stated that he knew his speech would be unacceptable to Republicans, but he did not care. Blacks in the state needed to know that it was more realistic to support the Democrats, and racial unity was imperative for the proper economic growth of the state. "The whites had the education, owned the land, and the capital. The black man owned the labor, and it was easy to see that it was the interest of both races to go hand in hand together."[36]

The avowed nationalist declared that the Republicans had duped blacks into thinking that Democrats were evil. Moreover, many Afro-Americans acted as though the Republicans were the only guardians of the people's rights. They had to realize that the slaves were set free by democratic principles, which were not the exclusive preserve of Republicans; Democrats also upheld such principles. Hence, Delany advised freedmen not to support the Republicans in the state or national election of 1874 because they had exploited Afro-Americans. He cited the Republican failure to enact a Civil Rights Bill and Congressional approval of an educational qualification for jury duty as evidence of Republican efforts to limit the civil and political rights of Afro-Americans.

Delany's State House speech in September 1874 was crucial. It marked a turning point in his thought about the role of blacks in Reconstruction politics. Shortly thereafter the Honest Government League held a mass meeting in Charleston's Military Hall where he gave another speech. He repeated his theme of racial political unity, and again castigated the Republicans. He advised all *good* Democrats and Republicans in South Carolina, black and white, to support the work of the Honest Government League, and he asked the league to develop a broad platform that would represent the interests of both races. The emphasis on racial unity in state politics was received enthusiastically by the audience at Military Hall. Moreover, from that moment on, Delany looked more attractive to Democrats who had planned to remove the Republicans from political power in the state.

The integrationist tone in Delany's speeches assured him a position on the ticket for a state third party movement, which was a coalition of Independent Republicans and some Democrats. For the 1874 gubernatorial election, the new coalition nominated Judge John T. Green for governor and Delany for lieutenant governor. As he campaigned in the state, the *News and Courier* recorded a favorable but condescending reaction to his speeches: "It is a surprise and gratification to the whites to hear wise, generous and statesmanlike words from the lips of a black man, and the colored people are proud to see that a man of their own race can worthily stand side by side with Kershaw and McGowan in the advocacy of fair dealing and peace. Major Delany has, by his good work, strengthened the cause of honesty and reform."[37] Three days later the reporters of the paper noted that Delany's articulate speeches began to shatter the rigidity of Democrats toward biracial tickets. Unfortunately, once more Delany was denied a high political office. In the 1874 state elections, Daniel H. Chamberlain became governor, and Delany was defeated by the incumbent black lieutenant governor, Richard H. Gleaves.

When Delany ran for lieutenant governor, he was sixty-two years of age. He had not only aged chronologically, but his association with the Honest Government League indicated that his nationalism had waned too. He no longer spoke about his people pursuing a destiny in the South independent of whites. In fact, Delany had mellowed so much ideologically in the *New York World* he was identified as "a conservative Negro from South Carolina."[38] In the spring of 1875, however, William Cullen Bryant, Peter Cooper, and others invited

Delany to New York to lecture on race relations in the South. Speaking on "The Present Political Issues of the South," he claimed that northerners often had a distorted view of race relations in the region, and they had led the freedmen to believe "that democracy meant slavery and republicanism meant freedom," but freedmen were aware that many Republicans were carpetbaggers.[39] Delany ended his speech by assuring New Yorkers that a race war in the South was not imminent. Afro-Americans knew that an overt struggle was suicidal because whites outnumbered them seven to one. He insisted that there was no antagonism between the races in the region; the presence and actions of white northerners there precipitated it. Thus, Delany's New York speech was further evidence that he had drifted away from his customary extreme nationalistic posture as he had grown older.

The veteran nationalist's ideological mellowing came at an opportune time for the Democrats in South Carolina. By 1875, a low point for radical Reconstruction had been reached. President Grant had relaxed political restrictions on the conservatives, and they had begun to challenge black politicians. The Charleston *News and Courier* warned that Afro-American leaders would have to prove that they had qualities other than a black skin to retain political posts. This warning partly explained Delany's emphasis on an alliance between blacks and Democrats. He felt that the conservative threat would become the new political reality if Afro-Americans did not sever their ties with the northern-based Republican party. Delany's fears of political disaster for his people largely motivated his close association with conservative Democrats between 1876 and 1878.

At the beginning of 1876 the Charleston Democrats issued a sterner warning to carpetbaggers, scalawags, and black Republicans: rather than submit to domination by these forces, they would die fighting them. They argued that the color line was not being drawn by them, but by the radical Republicans and their Afro-American supporters. Hence, they advocated a return to southern white political domination. The conservatives did not care for an amalgamation of black and white political power, even though they spoke of developing a broad platform that would appeal to the voters of both races. They knew that some freedmen would not give up their Republican affiliation, but they were certain that many blacks would work with the Democrats for a new state government.[40]

The years 1875 and 1876 were turbulent for Delany. As he became more involved with Democrats, he had to endure public embarrassment precipitated by his Republican enemies. He was appointed a judge for Charleston's Third Ward in 1875, and it was reported that he was a model jurist. His chambers were clean, well furnished, and appropriately organized for court procedures; he even had an inner office for private consultations. Simultaneous with his new position, however, Delany was accused of embezzling $212 from the John Wesley Methodist Church of John's Island. When arraigned, he posted $1000 bail. He denied the charge, but stated that the case gave him the opportunity openly to refute the "lie."[41] Meanwhile Delany continued to serve as a judge.

Delany's trial was held at Charleston's Court of Sessions on 8 February 1876. He admitted taking the $212, but explained the circumstances of the case. Apparently the trustee who held the church's funds died, and his widow asked Delany what she should do with the money. He agreed to hold it for her, but surreptitiously invested it in some county claims. When the trustees demanded payment, they refused to take the claims from Delany. The defense lawyer, E. B. Seabrook, argued that, as a trustee of the estate of the late treasurer of the church, Delany "had made an unfortunate investment." He claimed also that the charge against Delany was politically motivated. The prosecutor denied the latter charge and proceeded to castigate Delany. After hearing both sides of the case, the jury deliberated ten minutes before it found Delany guilty. He was sentenced to one year in prison, but was released on a $1000 bond.[42]

To keep Delany from being imprisoned, a group of black citizens in Charleston asked Governor Chamberlain for a pardon. The petitioners told the governor that Delany was one of the few men of their race of whom they could be proud. To prevent him from going to jail, they promised to pay the money to the church because Delany was one of the most venerated black citizens in America.[43] Even Republicans who opposed Delany felt that his sentence was too harsh. As it happened, Delany paid the $212 to the aggrieved church, and he was pardoned by Governor Chamberlain.

Delany's trial caused him much public embarrassment, but it did not deter him from being an able and fair judge. From the end of his trial to mid-June, Delany heard several cases in his court. Most of them were misdemeanors, mainly assault and battery. He always treated defendants fairly, and his even-handedness earned him the reputation of being a compassionate judge.[44] However, Delany's legal career lasted less than one year. On 23 July, the secretary of state informed him that the Senate had not confirmed him for another term.

After his brief stint as a trial justice, Delany returned to the practice of medicine and became involved in the gubernatorial election of 1876. The latter event provided him an opportunity to demonstrate the kind of political flexibility he had urged his people to adopt. At first he agreed to campaign for the re-election of Governor Chamberlain, a Republican. Delany felt that the governor would look out for the interests of blacks, but he did not trust other members of the party in the state. When the Republicans met in Columbia and voted to return the same group of men to office, Delany switched his support to the Democratic nominee, Wade Hampton. After mid-September he tried to persuade his people to vote for the Democrats.

Delany knew that conservative control of state politics was inevitable, but he had hoped his people's political rights would be preserved if they cooperated with the Democrats; meanwhile he upbraided them for being complacent in a time of crisis. For instance, in a keynote address at a fourth of July celebration attended by nearly 10,000 black Charlestonians, Delany spent most of his time cataloguing their shortcomings. If they persisted in their immorality, lack of education, and poor social conditions, he warned, they would not be able to compete with whites or reach a high stage of development. Delany's candor stemmed from a genuine concern for his people's growth.

Delany worked with the Democrats in Charleston's Fourth Ward and in other parts of the state. At the time, conservatives in South Carolina were impressed with the cooperation between black and white Democrats in Virginia and North Carolina; both wanted Samuel J. Tilden to be elected president. This biracial effort prompted conservatives to launch a propaganda campaign to woo freedmen away from the Republicans. A lengthy editorial in the *News and Courier* reminded blacks that the Republicans had not kept their promises since emancipation. The dream of owning forty acres and a mule had not been realized, and Afro-Americans had received few benefits from Freedmen's Savings Bank. Although they were emancipated, blacks had become slaves to the Republican party. Then the freedmen were reminded that it was the whites in the state who employed them, not those from the North. Finally, it was suggested that economic reconstruction under Democratic leadership would benefit both races. In content, then, there was some similarity of views between the white conservatives and Delany, although the long-term goals were quite different. He wanted his people's rights preserved in the state after Reconstruction, but the Democrats really wanted to exclude them from the new political order.

At a Fourth Ward Democratic Club meeting on 14 September, Delany explained why Afro-Americans should have voted for the Democratic ticket in 1876. He asserted that the Fifteenth Amendment tacitly made all Afro-Americans Democrats because the right to vote implied the right to rule. Thus, blacks in the state needed to be more flexible politically. They needed to vote for men who would serve their best interests, whether such men were Republicans or not. Meanwhile, blacks expressed their dissatisfaction with Delany's association with conservative whites. When he ventured to speak for the Democrats at Edisto Island, the freedmen there said they did not care to hear a "Nigger Democrat." Delany retorted that he had been to England and Africa but "he had never been insulted as he had been today by the people of his own race."[45]

Later Delany and a black teacher from Charleston, W. J. McKinlay, campaigned with Democrats at Cainhoy. When his associate rose to speak, a group of black Republican sympathizers fired at the assembly and killed some of the black and white spectators. According to the *News and Courier*, black Republicans were angry with Delany because he supported the Democrats, and they wanted to kill him. Delany and others escaped death only when they hid in a church nearby. In an editorial in the *News and Courier*, the Cainhoy incident was called "unprovoked butchery . . . by black savages," and the writer suggested that Charleston would soon become a "theatre of horrors that would disgrace Ashantee."[46]

Violence had spread throughout the state by 1876, but most of it was the work of whites, not blacks. The Democrats rallied all of their resources to wrench political control from the Republicans. They used various methods to force blacks to vote for *their* party or not to vote at all. Hampton's Red Shirts (rifle clubs) brandished their weapons at parades and the political meetings of both parties to intimidate the electorate, and the Democrats often stuffed ballot boxes.[47] Delany was ominously silent about these tactics. He was so enraged at the Republicans that he overlooked the undemocratic practices of the Democrats. During his affiliation with them, Delany had persuaded many freedmen to vote for Wade Hampton. His efforts helped Hampton, a former Confederate general, to be elected governor in 1876. Yet under his administration, the Democrats purposely disfranchised Afro-Americans in the state. What happened in South Carolina was typical of all southern states. Conservatives proceeded to exclude blacks from a substantive role in political and economic developments. The reaction prompted hundreds of blacks to leave the South. Some migrated to midwestern states, and many were ready to emigrate to Africa. The latter interest provided Delany with his last opportunity to become involved with a pan-African movement.

8

Pan-Africanism Reconsidered

Delany never had lost his interest in Africa. Some time after the destruction of his private papers in 1864, he wrote about the continent with a new urgency. In a polemical essay entitled "The International Policy of the World Towards the African Race," Delany sought to expose prevalent racial myths about Africa. First, he dealt with the question of slavery. He charged that European apologists jusified racial slavery by claiming that blacks were inferior to whites. Such sophistry overlooked the fact that Anglo-Saxons once were slaves, and that the Russian nobility did not emancipate the serfs until 1864. Yet these white servile classes were not considered to be incapable of being civilized. Slavery had been institutionalized in many parts of Europe in ancient and medieval times, but "as civilization advanced" in that sector of the world, it became more difficult to justify the practice. Hence, on the eve of modern history Europeans were embarrassed by the enthrallment of their own people, and Delany believed that they purposely had sought non-European peoples to subjugate. "For this dreadful purpose the African was selected as the victim of an international conspiracy. A political conspiracy of malice aforethought, prompted by avarice and the love of lucre."[1]

Because of the rape of Africa and the enslavement of four million of its sons and daughters in the South, Delany decided it was time for a black leader to expose the "lie" that Africans were inferior, and reveal how this racial falsehood began. Seeing himself as the tireless defender of the honor of the African race, Delany vowed to uncover the European plot that denigrated his people: "I should not feel, whatever I may have effectively done, that my work had been more than half completed, did I not, as a wronged and outraged son of Africa, give to the world this crowning act of infamy against a people, the facts of which have ever been closely concealed, and even denied, while thousands of the world's good people have no knowledge that such facts ever transpired."[2] With this declaration, Delany proceeded to present his version of the European conspiracy against Africa.

He was certain that African development had not equaled modern Europe because whites had "invaded" Africa to undermine its political, economic, and social systems. This scheme began when European navies, merchants, missionaries, and consuls moved among Africans near the coast "sowing the seeds of discord, and a baser corruption among the already corrupted natives, inciting them to war, and the devastation of their homes." Hence a deliberate European coastal presence and a calculated penetration into the interior of Africa precipitated a period of decadence on the continent.[3]

Having begun this decline, whites proceeded to postulate the view that Africans had made no noteworthy accomplishments; whatever achievements had occurred in Africa were the result of the initiative and genius of caucasoid peoples who migrated there.[4]

Delany attempted to counteract the European interpretation of Africa's development by reviewing its early history from a black perspective. In his essay he protested that the first Egyptians were black men, and they were the greatest men of ancient times. The avowed pan-Africanist admitted that the Arabs had made contributions to world civilization by formulating an arithmetical system and various philosophical concepts, but he believed they did not surpass the Africans in these categories. In fact, Delany claimed that the Arabs *stole* their ideas from the black Egyptians when they plundered the Museum of Alexandria. He insisted that ancient Africans had held lofty philosophical and religious beliefs, which caused them to display a reverence for the supernatural and permitted them to develop a high degree of pure ethics. Because of their intensive contemplation of such ideas, black men had become the most tolerant and religious human beings.

Delany's criticism of the European view of African development was significant, particularly because he contended that the black man's contribution to world civilization was his humanism. It allowed him to survive in a hostile world and to embrace the social and religious institutions of any civilization; racism, however, had caused whites to view the African's adaptability negatively. They inevitably referred to the black man's ability to adjust to an alien culture as imitation. But to Delany this talent was really an innate quality which allowed Africans to endure any human condition. To support his argument, Delany referred to the African's ability to survive the ordeal of slavery in the United States and still hope for a glorious future thereafter.

Although the will of Afro-Americans for centuries had been "terribly crushed and shattered [their] true African character [had survived], these lurking faculties for higher attainments rising superior to the fetters which bound the body of the possessor, would occasionally burst forth like the sudden illumination of a brilliant meteor, startling the midnight gazer while all was enshrined in darkness around."[5]

After he had dealt with the generalization that Africans had few accomplishments, Delany questioned the assumption that there were many external influences on African culture. First, he argued that much of the political and religious symbolism of Middle Eastern and European peoples was of African origin. For instance, the idea that kings were the human embodiment of God was an African concept which evolved in ancient times. The ivory and gold thrones on which the Pharaohs sat represented their durability and purity, and the scepter denoted authority. These were some of the symbols that other peoples borrowed for the investiture of their kings. Second, Delany claimed that when the Jewish people were held as bondsmen by Africans, they acquired some of the latter's political and religious symbols and later used them in their anthropomorphic expressions of God. To illustrate this point, he referred to numerous expressions in the Old Testament Scriptures. God was a self-creating Being, a consuming fire, who sat on a white throne, and no man could look at Him and live.

Finally, Delany raised challenging questions about the architectural and orthographic achievements of the Egyptians. He asked, "Who were the builders of the everlasting pyramids, catacombs, and sculptors of the sphinxes? Were they Europeans or Caucasians, Asiatics or Mongolians? Will it be at once conceded that the author of the symbolic mythology and hieroglyphic science are identical? Upon this point there is but one opinion. The inventors or authors of the one were the builders or architects of the other."[6] If Asians or Europeans were the originators of the pyramids and hieroglyphics, Delany wanted to know why these phenomena were not distinct features of their cultures. To him it seemed illogical to say that others had given so much of their cultural features to Africans when such characteristics were not present in their own societies. Thus the European argument of African cultural borrowings was "preposterous." The architecture, religious and political symbolism, and hieroglyphics of the ancient Africans were distinctly African; alien invaders of Northeast Africa found these features in Egypt when they arrived. Delany concluded that Africans had developed a civilization when the Greeks were still uncivilized.

Delany believed that his interpretation of African history was justified. The notion of white supremacy was inimical to the advancement of his people, who would be helped by learning of their African heritage. They had to know that the development of black civilizations in Africa predated the slave trade era and European expansion on the continent. Moreover, Delany declared that his people had to realize that there was an international conspiracy to subjugate the whole African race. Delany's polemical essay was significant. It indicated that even after the failure of his pan-African movement, he intended to be a spokesman for Africa's regeneration.[7]

In 1878 Delany wrote his last monograph. It was entitled *The Principia of Ethnology: The Origin of Races and Color, with an Archaeological Compendium of Ethiopian and Egyptian Civilization, from Years of Careful Examination and Enquiry*. His main objective was to show that black men were equal to white men. The pan-African advocate was disturbed by contemporary works which assigned Africans last place among the three major races of the world. In 1850 Josiah Clark Nott, a southern ethnologist, and George R. Gliddon wrote *Types of Mankind*. Seven years later they published another book on the *Indigenous Races of the Earth*. In both works the authors opposed the theory that all men evolved from a common ancestor. They hypothesized that there were diverse races with separate origins. Moreover, Nott and Gliddon contended that "Negroes" never had produced a high civilization. Then in 1869 a prominent Scottish politicain, George John Douglas Campbell (the eighth Duke of Argyll), wrote a treatise on *Primeval Man*. In his treatise the duke claimed he knew about the beginning of the white and yellow races, but he was unable to account for the origin of the black race. Unlike these three authors, Delany believed in the unity of mankind, and contended that the Biblical version of human creation was more accurate than the ethnological theories of human evolution. Even if the origins of the three races were distinct, Delany implied that blacks were created first.[8]

Delany's monograph was really a literary supplement to his earlier polemical essay, and an effort to add "new" evidence to his thesis that Africans were the first civilized men. In the latest work, however, Delany contended that there was a definite link between human creation and African civilization. He believed all races evolved from one human ancestor, but God employed three agencies to disperse man throughout the earth and to foster the development of diverse civilizations. These agencies were "Revolution, Conquest, and Emigration."[9] For him, emigration was the most essential agent because it placed men in various geographical regions where they initiated progressive revolutions. Delany admitted there were violent revolutions, but he preferred nonviolent revolutions to promote civilization. The Tower of Babel and the Great Flood were catastrophic events designed to make man migrate from his original homeland. The deluge was significant because it caused the Hamitic migration into the northeastern region of the African continent. In his essay Delany doubted the European view of outside influences on Africa, but in his book he expressed no reservations about the Hamitic migration into Africa. He claimed that the Hamites were negroid, not caucasoid. They were among the ancestors of those ancient Africans who had built "imperishable monuments of their superior attainments" in Egypt, Sudan, and Ethiopia.

Toward the end of the book Delany suggested that it was important for contemporary blacks to recognize and appreciate the achievements of the ancient Africans. The Egyptians, Sudanese, and Ethiopians had reached a high stage of development because of the stability of their cultures. In modern times, however, Delany feared that continual white influences on black men everywhere would result in the cultural decay of the race. West Africans near the coast were corrupted already by their associations with Europeans, but people in the interior had maintained the traditional life style of their ancestors. Yet a growing European presence on the continent appeared imminent. Culturally, Delany felt that the future appeared bleak for new world blacks because acculturation and miscegenation greatly had diminished their African identity. The pan-African leader admitted that Africans had fallen behind Europeans in modern times. But a new initiative by black men in the motherland and the diaspora would assure the regeneraton of the race, and the theories about racial inferiority could not prevent its upward mobility.

Delany published his last monograph to coincide with the development of the Liberia exodus movement in Charleston. By the late 1870s hundreds of freedmen throughout the South talked of settling in Liberia. They wanted to leave America because they thought there was little hope for advancement in a region where they were disfranchised, economically deprived, and socially ostracized.[10] The disgruntled freedmen believed that in Liberia they would have political privileges, and the right to work out their own destinies. Many of them desired to go to Liberia under the sponsorship of the American Colonization Society, but a group of black leaders in Charleston felt that Afro-Americans needed to form their own independent, self-sufficient organization to transport freedmen to Liberia. Among them were H. N. Bouey, a probate judge from Edgefield County, and Rev. B. F. Porter, the pastor of Morris Brown A.M.E. Church in Charleston. These men shared the belief that the economic and political future for Afro-Americans was bleak, but perhaps in Africa they could achieve full manhood.

On 4 July 1877, Rev. Porter, Bouey, and other emigration enthusiasts met at Porter's church to form the Liberia Exodus Association. At the time, a Liberian citizen visiting Charleston, J. C. Hazeley, encouraged the new generation of emigrationists to pursue their goal vigorously. When the black citizens of Charleston held their Liberia Independence Day celebration 26 July, Rev. Porter told the audience at Hampstead Hall that the association planned to form a joint stock company. He noted that there were 400,000 Afro-Americans in South Carolina. If 30,000 of them purchased stocks at $10.00 a share, the association would have $300,000 to send emigrants to Liberia. A portion of the money would be used to buy a ship and to outfit it for a trip to Liberia in November.[12] Porter's public appeal was partly successful, and the Liberia Exodus Joint Stock Steamship Company was incorporated as a subsidiary firm of the Liberia Exodus Association.

By October 1877 65,000 freedmen had registered with the Liberia Exodus Association, but it had sold only 100 shares of stock.[13] Encouraged by the large membership who expressed a desire to emigrate, Rev. Porter wrote the president of Liberia, Rev. James S. Payne, for permission to send freedmen there. He said, "We come pleading in the name of our common Father that our beloved brethren and sisters of the Republic . . . will grant us a home with you and yours in the land of our Fathers . . . where we can live and aid in building up a nationality of Africans, we will come, and in coming we will be prepared to take care of ourselves and not be burdensome to the Government."[14] In addition to permission to settle in Liberia the association asked the government of Liberia to billet emigrants until they were permanently located on tracts of land provided by the government.

On 21 December 1877, Liberia's Congressional Committee on Immigration sent an affirmative reply to the Liberia Exodus Association. The committee informed the association that the government had no public housing, but temporary quarters would be found for the emigrants. It promised to let the freedmen settle in the counties of Montserrado, Grand Bassa, Sinoe, and Maryland, all of which were fertile and well-watered. The Liberian Congress said it would welcome freedmen from Charleston, but was candid about what the newcomers should expect in Liberia. They had to be willing to endure hardships while they adjusted to the people and the country, and they had to have the "desire to assist in erecting a Christian Negro Empire."[15] If the freedmen accepted these conditions, the government promised to give each family twenty-five acres of land. If they wanted more land, they would have to pay the government fifty cents an acre.

By January 1878 the financial status of the association's joint stock company had improved; net assets now were $6000. Although this was far short of the projected goal of $300,000, the association purchased the *Azor*. This initial debt was the beginning of a financial crisis that destroyed the Liberia Exodus Association. The *Azor*, built originally to carry slaves, had been converted to a cargo ship carrying products from the Azure Islands to Boston, Massachusetts. When the association purchased it, the ship had made ninety-nine voyages across the Atlantic.

The "christening" of the *Azor* in Charleston harbor on 21 March 1878 was a momentous occasion. Rev. Porter saw the dedication of the *Azor* as evidence that Afro-American Christian men at last had accepted their evangelical responsibility toward Africa, and Bishop Morris Brown and Rev. Henry M. Turner, a pan-African advocate, repeated this theme in their speeches. The religious significance of the *Azor*'s mission to Liberia was reflected in the composition of its passengers. When the ship left Charleston 21 April 1878, there were two congregations among the 256 emigrants. There was an A.M.E. group led by Rev. S. Flegler as well as a group from the Shiloh Baptist Church, which included seven deacons but no pastor.[16] In addition, the American and Foreign Bible Society provided the emigrants with one hundred Bibles, and the American Baptist Publication Society gave them Sunday School texts. Because of the large number of church members among the emigrants, Rev. Turner classified the *Azor* as a "black Mayflower": "It was not only to bear to Africa a certain number of her sable sons and daughters, it was not only to bear a load of humanity but to take back the culture, education and religion acquired here. The work inaugurated then would never stop until the blaze of Gospel truth should glitter over the whole broad African continent."[17]

While many viewed the maiden voyage of the *Azor* as a miraculous event, tragedy struck before it reached Monrovia. The *Azor* left Charleston 21 April 1878, but twenty-two of its passengers died from drinking polluted water before the ship reached Freetown, Sierra Leone on 19 May. Despite these deaths, the morale of the emigrants was high, and at Freetown the captain acquired supplies before proceeding to Liberia. The *Azor* finally arrived at Monrovia on 3 June, and all of its passengers (including the two babies born during the voyage) had disembarked by 5 June. The emigrants received a cordial welcome from Monrovian officials, but they did not proceed to Boporo as planned. Most of them settled at Digby, northwest of Monrovia. Others moved to the village of Dixville near New Georgia, and some remained in Monrovia. After its passengers had been discharged, the *Azor* left for Charleston on 24 July without passengers or a cargo.

Until the summer of 1878 Delany was not a prime mover in the Liberia exodus movement. Rev. Porter, H. N. Bouey, and other leaders recognized him as the chief advocate of emigration to Africa, and they appointed him as chairman of the finance committee of the Liberia Exodus Joint Stock Steamship Company. Since the leaders of the company did not receive salaries, Delany devoted most of his time to his medical practice in Charleston. Once the company had incurred debts in Freetown and Monrovia, the board of the Liberia Exodus Association asked him to play a more active role to help them defray their expenses, and he complied. The association was established as an independent, self-sufficient emigration organization, but in the summer of 1878 it tried to solicit aid from the American Colonization Society. When Delany agreed to cooperate with this new policy, it marked a significant departure in his pan-African ideology; he hoped his activities would help him to return to Africa.

In the 1850s Delany had refused to associate with colonizationists, and he saw Liberia as their colony. By the 1870s, however, much had changed. Liberia had emerged as an independent state less reliant on the American Colonization Society. Moreover, after his unsuccessful attempt to gain a key political post in South Carolina, Delany had hoped to fulfill his dream of returning to Africa by being appointed the United States Minister to Liberia. Ironically, William Coppinger was the head of the Pennsylvania Colonization Society in 1859 when it helped Robert Campbell to go to Yorubaland. At that time, Coppinger was one of the men Delany referred to as an enemy of the emigrationists. In 1878, however, Coppinger ran the Washington office of the American Colonization Society, and Delany thought Coppinger might be able to use his influence with the government to award him the Liberia appointment. These were the main reasons why Delany had agreed to cooperate with colonizationists in the last decade of his life.

At first Delany corresponded with J. H. B. Latrobe, the president of the American Colonization Society, to acquaint him with the reasons for the development of the Charleston exodus movement. Like Delany, the leaders of the Liberia Exodus Association held the view that Afro-Americans were an alien race in the United States with little hope of advancement. Hence, the freedmen's voluntary exodus to Africa was psychologically and morally correct. They were certain that the exclusion of blacks from the mainstream of southern society would make them a spiritless people, and force their children to become "an indolent, indifferent, idle set of creatures, a social pest upon the body politic."[18] The new emigrationists also believed that the limited economic opportunities for the freedmen made the exodus movement imperative. They were perturbed by the influx of Europeans in the North and the South. They were certain that Afro-American unemployment would be the logical consequence of European immigration. This trend contributed to the growing surplus black labor force in the South; they could not emigrate north without antagonizing white workers there. Hence, if America could relieve Europe of its population pressures, it was not wrong for Africa to absorb the victims of economic discrimination.

Since the American Colonization Society and the Liberia Exodus Association transported Afro-Americans to Liberia, Delany told Latrobe that he saw no reason why they could not cooperate. Specifically, Delany asked Latrobe if the ACS would loan the joint stock company $1680 to cover the cost of the provisions acquired at Freetown and the towing charges from there to Monrovia. Delany was certain his firm could repay the loan by November because it expected more freedmen to buy stocks after they had harvested and sold their fall crops. In his usual manner when dealing with whites, Delany told Latrobe that the association wanted a loan, not a donation, because the "movement is intended to be self-sustaining in order to make our people self-reliant."[19]

After Latrobe considered Delany's suggestion of cooperation, and the loan, he decided that the ACS should be cautious when dealing with the exodus movement from Charleston because he feared antagonism might develop between the two organizations. He advised William Coppinger to consider Delany's offer and merely express sympathy with it until the board of directors of the ACS had an opportunity to look into the matter. Latrobe's reluctance to aid the Charleston exodus movement prompted Rev. Porter and Rev. Cain to visit the president of the ACS at his home in Baltimore, Maryland, to see if he would not reconsider his position. Cain was conciliatory, but Porter was bold. He let Latrobe know that, despite all obstacles, the Liberia Exodus Association intended to take more emigrants to Liberia. Latrobe was not disturbed by Porter's determination. He concluded that regardless of what others thought about the ACS, the society was doing its share to provide a home in Africa for Afro-Americans.

With no assurance of a loan from the American Colonization Society, the exodus association contacted the Pennsylvania Colonization Society. On 17 July 1878, Delany wrote the president, Eli K. Price, for a loan of $2000. To repay it, the exodus steamship company would carry the Pennsylvania society's black clients to Liberia for a lower price than that charged by Yates and Porterfield, the New York shipping firm which carried all colonizationist passengers to Africa. Yates and Porterfield charged $100 for cabin passengers and $50 for steerage. But Delany offered the same accommodations on the *Azor* for $65 and $25 respectively. If the Pennsylvania society did not care for the arrangement, the exodus firm would use the *Azor* as security for the loan. After Delany's initial enquiry, Rev. Porter pleaded with Price to help the exodus movement. He sympathized with the plight of the black steamship company, but said his society would follow the policy of the ACS.[20]

Colonizationists refused to help the Liberia Exodus Joint Stock Steamship Company because they saw it as a rival organization. Latrobe thought the new emigrationists would challenge the preeminence and influence of the ACS in Liberia, and its authoritative position among Afro-Americans who wanted to go there.[21] John Orcutt, an agent for the society, advised its directors not to accede to Delany's request for a loan because a benevolence organization held funds in trust and could not assist a business venture. Moreover, the emigration plans of Delany and his associates were too elaborate to assure success; unlike the society, the exodus group had not learned how to "make haste slowly." They needed to plan to take smaller groups of emigrants periodically, and "wait for the development of providence in the case."[22] Orcutt concluded that neither "justice or mercy" demanded that the colonizationists should help the emigrationists, for the failure of their enterprise was inevitable.

Isaac S. Smith, treasurer of the New York Colonization Society, disagreed with the positions of Latrobe and Orcutt. He contended that, although the ACS opposed the leaders of the South Carolina exodus movement, it had a humanitarian obligation to assist the emigrants they sent to Liberia. J. B. Pinney, secretary of the New York Colonization Society, had reported from Liberia that there was a shortage of medical supplies in the country. Since the society provided these supplies, it was imperative that they share them with the emigrants from South Carolina. At the same time, the society should warn the Liberia Exodus Association to send its people medical provisions. If the society took these affirmative actions, it would feel no guilt if the South Carolina movement failed.[23] Later Smith told Coppinger that he saw nothing wrong with allowing the South Carolinans to use the society's hostel in Monrovia when it was vacant. Smith's opinions carried little weight with the American Colonization Society, which maintained a policy of indifference to the Liberia Exodus Association.

Although colonizationists were unhappy with the development of the exodus movement in Charleston, they did not deny its impact on freedmen in the South. It was estimated that at least 500,000 Afro-Americans were sympathetic to the movement.[24] Indirectly, the society saw the exodus movement as a vindication of its colonization scheme. If it had not established Liberia, Afro-Americans may not have found a place of refuge in the motherland. The colonizationists were willing to take credit for any success that the Liberia Exodus Association had, but they disclaimed any association with, or responsibility for its failures. It attributed the twenty-two deaths on the *Azor* to poor preparation by the association. By contrast, the society's transportation record was an enviable one. By 1878, ships had taken its passengers across the Atlantic 160 times. The colonizationists were certain that the *Azor*'s first voyage was marked by tragedy because the emigrationists failed to heed their advice to "hasten slowly."[25]

Colonizationist opposition and criticism of the Charleston exodus movement did not discourage its leaders. They planned to send the *Azor* back to Liberia on 20 February 1879, with 150 emigrants and a cargo of goods produced by southern blacks.[26] This second voyage was not undertaken because the Liberia Exodus Joint Stock Steamship Company could not solve its financial problems. Without the loan from the colonizationists the firm was discredited in Sierra Leone. When the *Azor*'s captain, W. E. Holmes, sued the company for $6000 in unpaid claims, the Court of Admiralty in Charleston impounded the ship until the case was settled.[27] Furthermore, the humanitarianism of the emigrationists contributed to their financial crisis. After 256 emigrants had boarded the *Azor* on 21 April 1878, 300 freedmen were left on the docks of Charleston, and the joint stock company paid for their lodging and meals until they found jobs. Hence, by early 1879, the black steamship company was reorganized and Delany placed in charge of its financial affairs.

From April to November 1879 Delany devoted most of his time and energies to solving the problems of the Liberia Exodus Association. He noted that its joint stock company met with difficulties because the young leaders of the association lacked business experience. The veteran emigrationist dealt mainly with the captain's suit against the firm. The Admiralty Court ruled that most of the claims of the captain were extortionate, and they were reduced from $6000 to $2500. When the court ordered the sale of the *Azor* to pay the debt, Delany persuaded Charleston merchant E. Willis to assume the debt and become the agent for the joint stock company. The *Azor* was completely overhauled, and it was used for coastal trade between Baltimore and Charleston. It carried phosphate rock to Baltimore and returned with hay and corn. By the winter of 1879, Delany had repaid Willis the debt on the *Azor*, and it belonged to the exodus leaders once more.

Because of their financial problems, the Liberia Exodus Association reluctantly had used the *Azor* for commercial purposes in 1879, but the leaders were anxious to return to the original purpose of carrying emigrants to Liberia. Once again they attempted to gain the American Colonization Society's cooperation. Willis assured Coppinger that the association's joint stock company was sound, and it would be solvent by the winter of 1880, "but they [stood] in need of friendly aids and a helping hand from those who sympathized with the objects of their organization."[28] Willis tried to induce the colonizationists to use the *Azor* to carry some of their wards to Liberia until there was another contingent of exodus emigrants ready to go. The emigrationists were so eager to send the *Azor* back to Africa that they were willing to take passengers from the colonizationists at a reduced rate. Yates and Porterfield refused to pick up fares at any port south of New York unless they were paid an extra fee. But the emigrationists offered to collect anyone bound for Liberia through the society at any port from Charleston to New York for $50 each. The colonizationists continued to express their regrets for the plight of emigrationists, but maintained their policy of non-assistance.

By early 1880 the Liberia Exodus Association made some changes in its personnel. Delany no longer wanted to serve in an official capacity, but he remained a member because he assumed that his complete withdrawal would be a psychological blow to the movement. He allowed the steamship company to put his name on their new circular as the "late Acting President" until May 1880.[29] The new president-elect was F. J. Pugh. Then Delany's son, St. Cyprian, was appointed clerk for the steamship company. However, none of these changes seemed to improve the status of the exodus movement. The circular that the new "regime" published contained the conditions for emigration, including the cost of passage and adequate supplies for the first six months in Liberia. This more detailed information came too late. By the summer of 1880 prospective emigrants had lost confidence in the Liberia Exodus Association and began once more to look to the American Colonization Society to take them to Africa.

The Charleston exodus movement was not a complete failure. Although it passed into obscurity after 1880, people in the North and the South discussed the significance of the *Azor*'s maiden voyage to Liberia. This historic journey evoked romantic thoughts about the motherland among freedmen in the South. For instance, in a letter to William Coppinger, Abraham Burke included a poster for Liberia Independence Day celebrations, 28 July 1879, in Savannah, Georgia. The festivities for the occasion were prepared by a local Afro-American organization, the American Union Ethiopian Association. The motto for the affair was "Africa, Sweet Africa! The Land of our Ancestors." A song was written to commemorate Liberia's anniversary, and the last stanza contained a reference to the *Azor*.

> Oh, here the bark of *Azor* lies,
> In Africa, sweet Africa,
> To carry every native prize,
> To Africa, sweet Africa,
> Oh, listen now my native band,
> Let us go to that Happy Land,
> And we shall join our ancestor's band.
> In Africa, sweet Africa.[30]

Approximately 3000 freedmen attended the exercises on 28 July. Rev. J. S. Haines of Charleston, South Carolina, gave the keynote address in which he spoke optimistically of the continuation of the exodus movement.

The Liberia exodus movement marked the formal beginning of the missionary work of the A.M.E. Church in Africa. It started with Rev. Flegler's Liberia Mission group of the *Azor*. This congregation of thirty persons was organized at Morris Brown A.M.E. Church, Charleston, South Carolina, by Bishop John M. Brown and Rev. A. T. Carr. When the *Azor* reached Liberia, Rev. Flegler's people settled in Brewersville, where they built a mission and called it Bethel. When Rev. Flegler returned to the United States in 1881, S. J. Campbell and Clement Irons supervised the work.[31] On 23 November 1891, the Liberia Missionary Conference was organized, and it became a part of Bishop Henry McNeil Turner's Twelfth Episcopal District, which included Michigan, Ontario, Nova Scotia, Bermuda, Sierra Leone, San Domingo, Haiti, and Demerara. Today the A.M.E. Church carries on missionary work in eleven African countries: Liberia, Sierra Leone, Ghana, Nigeria, the Republic of South Africa, Lesotho, Swaziland, Mozambique, Zambia, Rhodesia, and Malawi.

The missionary outreach of the A.M.E. Church evolved from Bishop

Turner's pan-Africanism. Among Afro-American pan-Africanists, he was Delany's successor.[32] Like Delany, Bishop Turner believed the ultimate goal of all Afro-Americans was their return to Africa. The black man's residency in the United States was temporary; it was merely the locus of their tutelage. After they had embraced Christianity and western learning, it was their solemn duty to return to the motherland. It was ordained by God. Bishop Turner said, "We will hear the voice of mysterious providence saying return to the land of your fathers."

To improve its image among Afro-Americans, and accelerate its campaign to take more of them to Liberia during Reconstruction, the American Colonization Society elected two black leaders to its board in 1876, Bishop Turner and Bishop Jabez T. Campbell, both A.M.E. clergymen.[33] When he learned of his election, Turner wrote a lengthy letter of acceptance to the ACS in which he expressed views similar to Delany's. He held that Afro-Americans would never realize a high political, social, and economic status in the United States, South America, or the West Indies. Only in Africa would black men have "a government and nationality of [their] own." God had reserved the continent for them, hence it was imperative for them to return there and contribute to the development of a "United States of Africa."[34]

As more and more of his countrymen prepared to emigrate to Africa at the end of Radical Reconstruction, Bishop Turner made public speeches advocating emigration to Liberia. In the spring of 1879 he was unable to attend the National Convention of Colored People in Nashville, Tennessee, but he printed his address entitled "Emigration: Is it Right or Expedient?" and had it distributed at the meeting. In his speech Turner made two major points that were pan-African in tone. First, like Delany, he believed Afro-American emigration to Africa was logical and just. Thus it was unforgivable for some black men to oppose it. They did so because they had inherited the white Americans' hatred for Africa. Too often, Turner argued, this prejudiced attitude stemmed from a lack of knowledge about the continent's potential. As Delany had done in his recent writings, Turner protested that Africa was first among the continents of the world. In ancient times it was a cradle for civilization while the western world slumbered.

In the second major point of his speech, Turner challenged the thesis that Liberia was a graveyard. He claimed that fewer black settlers in Liberia perished than whites who died in the first English colonies in America. Using the works of Leonard Bacon and George

Bancroft as historical sources, Turner noted that nearly all of the colonists who came to Jamestown in 1607 and Plymouth in 1620 had died before a year was out. Moreover, Liberia was no less healthy than many southern cities, where a variety of epidemics had taken a heavy toll of human lives by 1879. On the other hand, Turner did not see why the opponents of emigration to Africa focused so much attention on Liberia. "Liberia [was] but a speck upon the face of that unexplored continent."[35]

Finally, the exodus movement sent Liberia some productive citizens. Of the 256 emigrants who left on the *Azor* 21 April 1878, twenty-two died en route, twenty-seven died in Liberia by 1880, and sixteen returned to the United States.[36] H. N. Bouey, one of the leaders of the Liberia Exodus Association, settled with other emigrants at Royesville. Two years after their arrival they had cleared a heavily forested area, established farms, and were growing cassava, corn, potatoes, and other vegetables. They also built two churches, one Baptist and the other A.M.E., and a day school. From Arthington, Jackson Clark wrote his brother in South Carolina, 8 August 1880, and explained how he had benefited by emigrating to Liberia. Not only had his economic condition improved, but he also thought that the health of his family had improved. His "mother and father [were] looking and feeling better than when they left Charleston." Because of his good fortune, Clark told his brother that Liberia was the best place for black people to live.[37]

One of the most imaginative emigrants to go with the *Azor* group was Clement Irons. Because of his inventiveness, he had become a prominent citizen in Charleston. He invented the "Irons Cotton Gin," and it was reported that he had a great future in Charleston. Yet he took his family to Liberia and settled at Brewersville. In Liberia Irons opened a machinist shop, where he repaired coffee and rice mills and other machinery. Then he built the first steamship in Liberia, and launched it on the St. Paul's River in December 1888. In addition to his mechanical interests, Irons had a ten-acre farm where he grew a variety of vegetables and coffee as cash crops. Along with Irons, there were two other emigrants from Charleston who had reached positions of high esteem in Liberia. C. L. Parsons became Chief Justice of the Liberian Supreme Court, and Rev. David Frazier was elected to the Senate in 1891.[38] So, even though another pan-African movement had failed to gain momentum the emigrants that had reached Liberia were able to achieve some measure of success.

While the Charleston emigrants were making new strides in Liberia, Delany spent the remaining five years of his life trying to return to Africa. Perhaps he could have returned to the motherland long before 1880, but it became evident that year that he had not done so because of his devotion to his children. In Delany's mind, his desire to return to Africa and the welfare of his children were not mutually exclusive. He wanted them to receive a good education to make them more useful to their people's struggle. By 1880 Delany had saved little money because he refused to become a corrupt politician during Reconstruction. Yet he wanted his two youngest children to complete their education at Wilberforce University. Delany had returned to the practice of medicine, but he did not expect it to provide him with enough money to cover the expenses of his children's schooling and his return to Africa. Hence, from 1880 on Delany sought a public position that would have given him sufficient funds to educate his children and permit him to return to Africa. He thought he could accomplish both tasks if he had a government job that paid at least $2000 to $3000 a year. If he could earn this much money for two years, Delany reckoned that he would have the money to achieve his goals.[39]

At the time, Delany said he would accept the post of United States Ambassador to Haiti. However, he feared that John Mercer Langston would be offered the position if James A. Garfield won the presidential election in 1880, since both were from Ohio. He told William Coppinger an appointment to Liberia was another possibility, but he was reluctant to seek it because he planned to live in Africa permanently. However, when the incumbent United States Minister to Liberia, Rev. Henry Highland Garnet, died suddenly in January 1882, Delany vigorously campaigned for the position. While on an extensive lecture tour in Pennsylvania, Maryland, and Delaware, Delany corresponded continually with William Coppinger, imploring him to urge the Executive Committee of the American Colonization Society to support him for the post.[40] The president, J. H. B. Latrobe, felt that Delany was a worthy candidate and recommended him highly to Secretary of State Frederick T. Frelinghuysen. Once again, however, Delany lost an opportunity to return to Africa when the State Department announced that John H. Smyth of North Carolina would be the new Minister to Liberia. Smyth's appointment ended Delany's long quest to return to Africa.

At seventy years of age, with the last hope of returning to Africa shattered, Delany reluctantly returned to his medical practice in Charleston. In 1884 a Boston firm offered him a job as its agent for Central America. Because he became ill later that year, he was unable to accept the appointment and decided instead to spend his last years with his family at Wilberforce, Ohio.⁴¹ The years of struggle and agitation for the rights of his people in America and the proper recognition of Africa's potential had taken their toll. Delany was weak and senile. He died finally of a lung infection on 24 January 1885,⁴² two years before the birth of the West Indian pan-African advocate Marcus Garvey.

By the time he died, Delany had become a legendary figure. In the *Xenia Daily Gazette* it was stated that "many think him to have exceeded Frederick Douglass, in intellect, in his palmiest days. He has been the guest of rulers and potentates of high degree, has taken a leading part in politics and is the author of several valuable books."⁴³ In Charleston the *News and Courier* referred to Delany as "one of the most prominent Negroes in the country, and who was at one time something of a prominent figure in this State."⁴⁴ The part of the legend that gave him the greatest notoriety, however, was his association with Africa.

From the late 1870s to his death Delany continued to focus his attention on Africa. During these years he wanted Afro-Americans to develop a deeper appreciation for their motherland. Because of this pan-African consciousness, Delany firmly believed that he was an apologist for Africa's achievements and potential in a world determined to discredit its heritage and its people. If there was any possibility of this interest diminishing, the entrenched white racist regimes in the South indirectly kept it alive. Their efforts to subvert their former slaves precipitated the exodus "fever" among blacks in the region. When the Charleston exodus movement began in 1877, Delany was recognized as the leading African-oriented emigrationist. He felt that the neo-emigrationist leaders in Charleston were inexperienced, impatient young men, but he agreed to help them in their moment of difficulty. In 1880, however, Delany decided that the time had come for him to make a final effort to return to Africa. By this time, he had learned to appreciate Liberia's independence, which he once scorned, and hoped he could spend his last days there. Though Delany's dream of returning to Africa was never realized, his accomplishments as a pan-Africanist must be evaluated by what he *dared* to do and not by what he failed to do.

Epilogue

Delany was the foremost nineteenth-century Afro-American exponent of pan-Africanism. For more than thirty years he was associated with African-oriented movements or wrote about the regeneration of the black race. A contemporary observer, Bishop Alexander Payne, described Delany this way: "He was too intensely African to be popular, and therefore multiplied enemies where he could have multiplied friends by the thousands. Had his love of humanity been as great as his love for his race, he might have rendered his personal influence co-extensive with that of Samuel Ward in his palmiest days, or that of Frederick Douglass at the present time."[1] Although it made him unpopular, Delany maintained his interest in African themes and projects and thereby made contributions to pan-African thought.

Delany was first an aspirant of racial pan-Africanism. He felt that the only way that black men could overcome the destructive consequences of white racism was to assert a separate course of action for themselves; the two races were incompatible because the primary goal of whites was the subjugation of blacks. Hence from the 1840s on Delany tried to persuade Afro-American leaders to pursue a course of black self-determination. Afro-Americans had to see themselves as a distinct group of people in the United States whose cultural heritage was African, not European. Furthermore, it was imperative for them to work for racial solidarity between themselves, West Indians, and Africans. Afro-Americans also had to realize that the abolition of slavery was merely the beginning of Africa's regeneration, and nation-building on the continent was its logical conclusion.

Through his back-to-Africa movement in the 1850s, Delany hoped to actualize the principles he had enunciated in the previous decade. He believed his African scheme typified a new Africa, where black men from the diaspora and Africa would develop the natural resources of the continent and evolve new polities. This concept was Delany's contribution to the ideological aspects of pan-Africanism. He was convinced that if black men built modern states then white men would respect them. More significantly, Delany anticipated the conflict between the races in the twentieth century, and predicted that a regenerated Africa would thwart the complete domination of his race and gain a voice in international affairs.

By the 1870s, Delany had become an advocate of cultural pan-Africanism. While in Africa, he had admired the varied activities of the Yoruba people and expressed his satisfaction with all aspects of their culture. Based on his observations, Delany concluded that the durability of African traditions would assure the advancement of the black race. His faith in Africa's potential caused Delany to challenge the European generalization that Africans had not made any contribution to human progress. He contended that Africans were the first men, and they developed the first civilized state in human history. Egypt was the envy of the ancient world; therefore, Europeans and Middle Eastern peoples borrowed many of its cultural features. Moreover, Africans were the most humane of all men, and this humanism was also a contribution to civilization. Delany viewed the European interpretation of African history as a plot to negate Africa's glorious past. This was dangerous because Afro-Americans would learn little about positive developments in Africa before the slave trade. To avert this possibility, he claimed that black people needed to have their own version of African history. It would inspire them to look beyond bitter experiences in America to a new era of greatness for the race.

Delany never realized his dream of settling in Africa, and Afro-Americans did not accept his pan-African vision. To most of them Africa was a dark, remote place from which their ancestors came, a place to which they did not want to return. This attitude was the main obstacle to Delany's hope of cooperation between new world blacks and Africans. Most black leaders urged their people to resist Delany's overtures to return to Africa. Nevertheless, from the 1840s to the 1870s, Delany was the only one who consistently held a bright image of Africa before his people. Thus, he properly belongs to that elite group of nineteenth-century pan-African advocates, which includes Paul Cuffe, Edward Wilmont Blyden, Alexander Crummell, and Henry McNeal Turner.

Since the rise of nationalism in Africa, the Civil Rights movement in America, and the establishment of black studies programs, recent scholars have developed a keen interest in Delany's nationalistic and pan-African thought. Professor George Shepperson categorized Delany as "one of the major pre-Civil War Negro American exponents of the 'Back-to-Africa' dream."[2] Other scholars have included excerpts of Delany's writings in their anthologies on black thought and pan-Africanism,[3] and his *Report of the Niger Valley Exploring Party*, along with Robert Campbell's, has been republished.[4] They all pay tribute to Delany, a man who was far ahead of his time.

Appendix A
Report of the Establishment of a Periodical, To be the Organ of the Black and Colored Race on the American Continent*

Your Committee, to whom was referred the duty of enquiring into the expediency of establishing a literary periodical, which should at the same time be the organ of the National Board of Commissioners, would respectfully submit, that they have investigated the subject as thoroughly as the limited time allowed them would permit.

It is evident to every one that a well-conducted and well supported press, is a most potent instrument in the moral and intellectual culture, and elevation of any people. This is emphatically a reading age and country. Elaborate works, which in former ages were only within the reach of the wealthy few, by popular and cheap editions, are brought within the reach of the most humble individual, or the most limited purse. While reviews, magazines and newspapers cover the land, authors, editors, essayists and critics have become a numerous class and by no other class in an enlightened country, is so great an influence exerted upon the characters of their fellow men, and the future destinies of the race. Theirs is the silent influence which goes with the divine into his study, and dictates the character of the doctrines and precepts which he must impress upon the minds of his bearers; it mounts the rostrum with the creator, and paints each glowing period that rolls from his tongue; it enters the halls of legislation, and gives tone to the debates, and shapes the character of the

---

* From *Proceedings of the National Emigration Convention of Colored People: held at Cleveland, August, 1854* (Pittsburgh: A. A. Anderson, 1854).

enactments; it enters the school-house, and stamps its impress upon the enquiring mind of the child, and moulds the character of the rising generation; in the domestic circle and in every relation of life, its all-pervading influence is felt. It is the facility for the rapid spread of intelligence and communication of ideas, which principally distinguishes the civilization of the nineteenth century from all that have preceded it; and any movement which fails to secure a due share of this potent influence in its favor, will be always undervalued in public estimation. This, like all other great influences in this country, has been arrayed against the negro; and while both law and public sentiment have conspired to place him in such a position as to exclude him entirely from all the usual avenues of literature and science, and render it impossible for him to make any great proficiency in intellectual culture, the very fact that in these attainments he is inferior to the privileged class, who have every incentive to exertion, and every opportunity for improvement, is brought up as evidence of natural inferiority; thereby making the legitimate fruit of oppression the strongest argument in favor of the oppressor, and of perpetuating the oppression. In accordance with this spirit, every branch of learning has been subsidized for the express and avowed purpose of keeping the negro down, and preventing him from ever rising in the scale of humanity. For this purpose the whole power of the government must be used to prevent the abolition of negro Slavery, or the building up of black nationality anywhere. The World of God must be corrupted, and the evidence of the Church adduced to show that Slavery is a blessing, compatible with the exercise of the highest and purest Christianity; the well established facts of history must be falsified, and science must be suborned to prove that black is white, and that white is black; and to cap the climax, some American savans have given a practical answer to the question of the Prophet, "Can the Ethiopian change his skin?" by *proving* as they say, that the ancient Ethiopians belonged to the white race. But one more step is needed, and that, by the skill of American ethnologists, and the pure morals and strict virtue of American patriarch, is rendered comparatively easy, that is, to prove that the *modern* negroes, as well as the *ancient* ones, belong to the white race, and bring us back to the old-fashioned doctrine of the unity of the human species.

In spite of all the obstacles thrown in their way, many colored men in this literature and science which would be creditable to any class of men, under the most favorable circumstances; but for want of a proper sphere of action, have remained unknown, except in the immediate circle of their acquaintance. There has never yet been any fair exhibition of the literary and scientific attainments of the Negro race. In the literature of the whites, as well as in white society the negro is at a discount, and nothing can raise him in either, but occupying a manly independent position, attained by his own efforts.

There have been published in the United States some twenty different newspapers edited and conducted, most of them with marked ability, by colored men; all of which, with the single exception of Frederick Douglass' paper, after progressing for a longer or a shorter period, have been suspended for want of patronage. While, therefore, your committee have nothing to offer in relation to newspapers in the country conducted entirely by colored men, they would earnestly recommend the establishment of a periodical which while it shall be the organ of the Board of Emigration, shall be open to a fair and impartial discussion of all questions connected with the welfare progress and development of the Negro race; and that it should also be made a literary periodical, calculated to give a fair representation of the acquirements of the colored race. That to this end, some of the ablest colored writers in both hemispheres should be engaged as its regular contributors, and articles invited on the various branches of literature, science, art, mechanics, law, commerce, philosophy, theology, et cetera; and that all the articles shall be the productions of colored men, except such selections as may be useful in illustrating some of the fundamental principles of this organization. Your committee believe that the publication of such a work would effect an incalculable amount of good in various ways. It would bring the evidence of progress, in a manner that it could not be disputed; and by furnishing manifestations of talent on the part of a large number of colored persons, would have more effect than masterly productions by one or two individuals; at the same time that it would present to colored men of ability an inducement to write, which they do not now possess.

Your committee think that it should be made a standard and permanent work, capable of reflecting credit upon our race; and to this end would recommend that each number be stereotyped, so as to make it a permanent compendium and book of reference, to mark the progress and development of the race. Such a work, having a special duty to perform, should differ in some of its essential features from any of the other publications, the monthly magazines, and quarterly reviews of the day. Although we have no doubt that such a periodical can, in a very short time, be made to sustain itself, and pay a fair profit; yet to place its success beyond continuency, and to ensure its permanency, we would recommend that all its expenses be paid from, and all its receipts go into the regular fund of the

Board. While we could not in the smallest degree slight or disparage the Anti-Slavery cause, and while such a periodical must, from its very nature, be the most powerful and efficient of all anti-slavery instrumentalities, yet we would recommend that no piece be received merely for its anti-Slavery qualities, but only for its merit as a literary production. The fact that a considerable portion of its patrons, as well as contributors, will probably be from other countries, and that solid will doubtless predominate over light matter in its pages, together with economical reasons, show that it should be a quarterly. We, therefore, recommend for your adoption the following resolution:

Resolved, That the Board of Commissioners be authorized and instructed to establish a quarterly periodical, as the organ of this organization, (in accordance with the foregoing outline,) to be called the *Afro-American Depository*, or some other name equally suggestive of its character.

JAMES M. WHITFIELD,
J. THEODORE HOLLY,
WILLIAM LAMBERT.

Number of Executive Delegates to the 1854 Emigration Convention

States	Delegates
Pennsylvania	84
Ohio	25
Michigan	16
Canada	4
Rhode Island	1
New York	1
Indiana	2
Louisiana	2
Wisconsin	2
Missouri	1
Kentucky	1
Tennessee	1
Total	139

Source: Martin R. Delany, *Chief Commissioner, Africa, Official Report of the Niger Valley Exploring Party* (New York: T. Hamilton, 1861), p. 7.

The National Board of Commissioners, Executive Officers and Central Commissioners

Name	Office	State
Martin R. Delany	President	Pittsburgh, Pa.
Rev. William Webb	Vice-President	Pittsburgh, Pa.
Thomas A. Brown	Treasurer	Pittsburgh, Pa.
Edward R. Parker	Auditor	Pittsburgh, Pa.
Charles W. Nighten	Secretary	Pittsburgh, Pa.
Prof. Martin H. Freeman	Special Foreign Secretary	Philadelphia, Pa.

Committee on Domestic Relations

Samuel Bruce	Chairman	Pittsburgh, Pa.
Martin R. Delany		
Edward R. Parker		

State Commissioners

William C. Nell	Boston, Massachusetts
Charles Lenox Remond	Salem, Massachusetts
James M. Whitfield	Buffalo, New York
J. Theodore Holly	Buffalo, New York
Augustus R. Green	Cincinnati, Ohio
Philip Toliver, Jr.	Cincinnati, Ohio
William C. Munroe	Detroit, Michigan
William Lambert	Detroit, Michigan
Conway Barbour	Louisville, Kentucky
Rev. Richard Anderson	St. Louis, Missouri
Rev. Jordan Brown	St. Louis, Missouri
Richard Henderson	Richmond, Virginia
John E. Ferguson	Richmond, Virginia
Elder Peter A. H. Lowry	Nashville, Tennessee
Charles Barratt	Nashville, Tennessee
Jordan B. Noble	New Orleans, Louisiana
Rev. John Garrow	New Orleans, Louisiana
Henry M. Collins	San Francisco, Calif.
Orange Lewis	San Francisco, Calif.

Source: *Proceedings of the National Emigration Convention of Colored People: held at Cleveland, August, 1854* (Pittsburgh: A. A. Anderson, 1854), pp. 16–18.

Appendix B
Published Version of Delany's Treaty*

This Treaty made between his Majesty Okukenu, Alake, Somoye, Ibasorun; Sokenu, Ogunbonna and Atambala, Chiefs and Balogusn of Abbeokuta [sic] on the first part, and Martin Robison Delany and Robert Campbell of the Niger Valley Exploring Party, Commissioners for the African Race of the United States and the Canadas in America, on the second part, covenants.

Article 1. That the King and Chiefs, on their part agree to grant and assign unto the said Commissioners on behalf of the African race in America, the right and privilege of settling in common with the Egba people, on any part of the territory belonging to Abbeokuta [sic] not otherwise occupied.

Article 2. That all matters requiring legal investigation among the settlers be left to themselves, to be disposed of according to their own custom.

Article 3. That the Commissioners on their part also agree that the settlers shall bring with them as an equivalent for the privileges above accorded, intelligence, education, a knowledge of the arts and sciences, agriculture and other mechanic and industrial occupations, which they shall put into immediate operation, by improving the lands, and in other useful vocations.

Article 4. That the Laws of the Egba people shall be strictly respected by the settlers and in all matters in which both parties are

---

* From Frank A. Rollin, *Life and Public Services of Martin R. Delany* (Boston: Lee and Sheppard, 1868), pp. 307-8, and Robert Campbell, *A Pilgrimage to My Motherland: An Account of A Journey Among the Egbas and Yorubas of Central Africa, in 1859-60* (New York: T. Hamilton, 1861), pp. 143-45.

concerned, an equal number of Commissioners, mutually agreed upon shall be appointed, who shall have power to settle such matters.

As a pledge of our faith and the sincerity of our hearts, we each of us hereunto affix our hand and seal, this twenty-seventh day of December Anno Domini one thousand eight hundred and fify-nine.

          His mark X Okukenu, Alake
          His mark X Somoye, Ibashorun
          His mark X Sokenu, Balagun
          His mark X Ogunbonna, Balagun
          His mark X Atambala, Balagun
          His mark X Oguseye, Ariaba
          His mark X Agtabo, Balagun Ose
          His mark X Ogundemu, Ageoki
          M. R. Delany
          Robert Campbell

Witness
    Samuel Crowther, Junior

Attest
    Samuel Crowther, Senior

Notes

Chapter 1

1. Harold Cruse, *The Crisis of the Negro Intellectual* (New York: William Morrow and Company, 1967), p. 129.
2. For a more complete discussion of Shango's powers see J. Olumide Lucas, *The Religion of the Yorubas* (Lagos: C.M.S. Bookshop, 1948), p. 104; G. Parrinder, *West African Religion* (London: Epworth Press, 1961), p. 12.
3. G. W. Williams, *History of the Negro Race in America*, vol. 1 (New York: G. P. Putnam's Sons, 1883), pp. 180–81.
4. Chapters 1–23 and 29–31 were serialized in issues of the *Anglo-African Magazine* from January to July 1859. Chapters 24–28 and 32–74 were printed in that magazine's successor, the *Weekly Anglo-African*, from 26 November 1861 to May 1862. All of these extant chapters were brought together in a single volume and edited by Floyd J. Miller, *Blake or the Huts of America* (Boston: Beacon Press, 1970).

Chapter 2

1. In Delany's home state of Pennsylvania political inequality for blacks continued until 1870. See Edward Raymond Turner, *The Negro in Pennsylvania, 1639–1861*, (Washington, D.C.: American Historical Association, 1912), p. 89.
2. W. E. B. DuBois, *The Philadelphia Negro: A Social Study*, 2d ed. (New York: Benjamin Blum, 1967), pp. 25–30.
3. Vernon Loggins, *The Negro Author* (New York: Columbia University Press, 1931), p. 183; Philip S. Foner, *Frederick Douglass* (New York: The Citadel Press, 1969), p. 77; *Daily Morning Chronicle*, 11 September 1843.
4. The *Mystery* remained in operation until 1848 when the African Methodist Episcopal Church purchased it and renamed the paper the *Christian Recorder*. Only fragments of Delany's paper have survived. See Frederick G. Detweiler, *The Negro Press in the United States* (Chicago: University of Chicago Press, 1922), p. 43.
5. *Palladium of Liberty*, 15 May 1844.

6. *Frederick Douglass' Paper*, 18 November 1853.
7. *Cincinnati Morning Herald*, 17 April 1847. The article in this paper concerning Delany's trial was reproduced in the *Pennsylvania Freeman*, 6 May 1847. For more information on the case see the *Daily Morning Chronicle*, 31 March, 12, 23 April 1847.
8. *Cincinnati Morning Herald*, 17 April 1847.
9. The exact date for the dissolution of the Douglass-Delany partnership is not clear. Foner claims that it ended on 29 June 1848, but Rollin gives 1 June 1849 as the date for Delany's departure from the *North Star*. On the other hand, his name was on the masthead as co-editor until the 29 June 1849 issue. Thus it would appear that Delany ended his partnership with Douglass in the summer of 1849. See Foner, *Frederick Douglass*, p. 92; Frank A. Rollin, *Life and Public Services of Martin R. Delany* (Boston: Lee and Sheppard, 1868), p. 69; and the *North Star*, 29 June 1849.
10. *North Star*, 31 March 1848.
11. Ibid., 18 February 1848.
12. Delany was chairman of the business committee, Ibid., 29 September 1848.
13. Martin R. Delany, *The Condition, Elevation, Emigration, and Destiny of the Colored People of the United States* (Philadelphia: Published by the author, 1852), p. 201.
14. *North Star*, 28 April 1848.
15. Ibid., 26 May 1848.
16. Ibid., 2 June 1848.
17. Ibid., 14 April 1848.
18. Ibid., 14 July 1848.
19. Ibid., 18 February 1848.
20. Ibid., 15 September 1848.
21. Ibid., 5 October 1849.
22. Dr. Joseph P. Gazzam to Berkshire Medical School, 31 October 1850; seven doctors from Allegheny City and ten from Pittsburgh sent recommendations the same day. Dr. F. Julius LeMoyne sent a recommendation 6 November 1850. See Folder AA 1.20, Box 3, Harvard Medical School Archives (hereafter cited as HMSA).
23. Rev. A. W. Black to Berkshire Medical School, 9 November 1850; supporting statements by other clergymen were attached to this letter. Ibid.
24. Henry Childs to Dean Oliver Wendell Holmes, 12 December 1850. Ibid. Before Delany, Henry Roberts, a Liberian, applied for admission to Berkshire, but was denied entry when the medical students protested. This decision was reversed when the school was criticized by people in Massachusetts. In referring to the Roberts affair, Henry Bibb claimed that Berkshire's first black graduate "proved to the world that color is but matter, that mind makes the man." *Emancipator*, 15 December 1847.
25. The medical students sent a "Petition on Colored Students" to the Medical Faculty 10 December 1850. Folder AA 1.20, Box 3, HMSA. In a separate letter fifteen students told the faculty that they would enroll in another medical school if Delany, Snowden, and Laing remained for the 1851 term. For further support of the protesting students see the *Boston Journal*, 17, 19 December 1850.
26. Medical Faculty Meetings, 12, 13 December 1850. *Minutes and Records of the Harvard Medical School Faculty*, vol. 2, pp. 74–76.

Chapter 3

1. Robin W. Winks, *Canada and the United States: The Civil War Years* (Baltimore: Johns Hopkins University Press, 1960), p. 7.
2. Howard H. Bell, "Expressions of Negro Militancy in the North, 1840-1860," *Journal of Negro History* 45 (January 1960): 12-16.
3. Delany, *Condition, Elevation, Emigration, and Destiny*, p. 156.
4. *Liberator*, 21 May 1852. Delany's reply to Garrison is also printed in Carter G. Woodson, *The Mind of the Negro as Reflected in Letters During the Crisis, 1800-1860* (Washington, D.C.: Associated Publishers, 1926), p. 293.
5. Mary Ann Shadd, *A Plea for Emigration; Or, Notes of Canada West, in Its Moral, Social, and Political Aspect* (Detroit: George W. Pattison, 1852).
6. *Voice of the Fugitive*, 24 September 1851.
7. Ibid.
8. Ibid., 19 November 1851.
9. *Frederick Douglass' Paper*, 23 July 1852.
10. Delany, *Condition, Elevation, Emigration, and Destiny*, p. 27.
11. *Frederick Douglass' Paper*, 1 April 1853.
12. Ibid., 6 May 1853.
13. Delany, *Condition, Elevation, Emigration, and Destiny*, p. 45.
14. Ibid., p. 12.
15. Ibid., p. 183.
16. Carter G. Woodson, *A Century of Negro Migration* (Washington, D.C.: The Association for the Study of Negro Life and History, 1918), pp. 77-79; Carter G. Woodson, *Negro Makers of History* (Washington, D.C.: Associated Publishers, 1928), pp. 159-60, Howard H. Bell, "The Negro Emigration Movement 1849-1854: A Phase of Negro Nationalism," *Phylon* 20 (1959): 132.
17. *Frederick Douglass' Paper*, 26 August 1853; *Provincial Freeman*, 22 April, 27 May 1854.
18. For discussions of the convention see W. E. B. DuBois, *John Brown* (New York: International Publishers, 1962), p. 245; Benjamin Brawley, *A Social History of the American Negro* (New York: The Macmillan Co., 1921), p. 164; John Wesley Cromwell, *The Early Negro Convention Movement* (Washington, D.C.: The American Negro Academy, 1904), p. 40; and Bell, "The Negro Emigration Movement," p. 140.
19. *Frederick Douglass' Paper*, 26 August 1853.
20. Only approximate figures can be given for the attendance at the Cleveland Convention because neither Delany nor any other observer of the event gave the actual numbers at the conclave. In his *Chief Commissioner, Africa, Official Report of the Niger Valley Exploring Party* (New York: T. Hamilton, 1865), p. 6, Delany claimed 1600 attended the plenary sessions. And A. H. M. Kirk-Greene quotes the same figure in his article, "America in the Niger Valley," *Phylon* 23 (1962): 228. While the Cleveland newspapers do not state a figure for the plenary sessions, different accounts were given of the number of delegates who attended. The *Cleveland Morning Leader*, 25 August 1854, claimed there were 150 delegates, but William Howard Day reported in the *Daily Cleveland Herald*, 25 August 1854, that there were only 138 delegates present. When Delany lectured in Scotland, however, he gave the approximate figures cited in the text above, which were recorded by the *Glasgow Morning Journal*, 9 October 1860.

21. *Proceedings of the National Emigration Convention of Colored People: held at Cleveland, August, 1854* (Pittsburgh: A. A. Anderson, 1854), p. 21.
22. Ibid., p. 26-27.
23. While the *Proceedings* give the name of the men appointed to the first five positions in the Executive Department, the office of Foreign Secretary was left vacant in 1854. Ibid., p. 15.
24. Ibid., p. 75.
25. Ibid., pp. 40-41.
26. *Frederick Douglass' Paper*, 26 August 1853; Foner, *Frederick Douglass*, p. 123.
27. *Frederick Douglass' Paper*, 13 January 1854. A more complete copy of the *Call* was published by the editors of the *Provincial Freeman*, 15 April 1854.
28. *Frederick Douglass' Paper*, 28 October, 18 November 1853; 27 October 1854.
29. Ibid., 27 January 1854.
30. Ibid., 18 November 1853.

Chapter 4

1. *Frederick Douglass' Paper*, 25 November 1853.
2. James M. Whitfield, *America, and Other Poems* (Buffalo: James S. Leavitt, 1853), p. i.
3. *Proceedings of the National Emigration Convention*, p. 73.
4. *Chatham Weekly Planet*, 21 February 1861.
5. Cromwell, *Early Negro Convention Movement*, p. 44.
6. Rollin, *Life and Public Services of Delany*, p. 71.
7. Because of Delany's silence concerning replies to his inquiries to men in Latin American countries, one must assume that they were negative. See Delany, *Niger Valley Exploring Party*, p. 10.
8. *Provincial Freeman*, 5 July 1856.
9. Brion Gysin, *To Master—A Long Goodnight* (New York: Creative Age Press, 1946), pp. 163-64.
10. *Chatham Tri-Weekly Planet*, 14 December 1857.
11. Despite Canadian confidence about their lack of prejudice, segregation was obvious in many towns in Western Ontario. See Winks, *Canada and the United States*, p. 8; Fred Landon, "Social Conditions Among the Negroes in Upper Canada," *Ontario Historical Society Papers and Records* 22 (1925): 146-47.
12. A consideration of Delany's association with John Brown is important because it was suggested that he was a co-conspirator with Brown in his Harper's Ferry raid. Rollin, *Life and Public Services of Delany*, p. 94; *Chatham Tri-Weekly Planet*, 25 October 1859.
13. Osborne Perry Anderson, *A Voice from Harper's Ferry* (Boston: Printed by the author, 1861), p. 9.
14. *Chatham Tri-Weekly Planet*, 23 August 1858.
15. Delany, *Niger Valley Exploring Party*, p. 12; *Chatham Tri-Weekly Planet*, 22 September 1858.
16. J. B. Pinney to R. R. Gurley, 8 February 1859; Robert Campbell and William

Purnell to Harvey Lindsey, 17 February 1859, American Colonization Society Papers, 154, Library of Congress (hereafter cited as ACS Papers).
17. Pinney to Gurley, 15 April 1859, and Coppinger to Gurley, 22 April 1859, Ibid., 155.
18. Delany, *Niger Valley Exploring Party*, p. 15.
19. Coppinger to Gurley, 4 April, 22 April 1859, and Pinney to Gurley, 15 April 1859, ACS Papers, 155.
20. Delany, *Niger Valley Exploring Party*, p. 15.
21. In his 1852 work Delany used extensive quotations from the journals of Denham and Clapperton. Delany, *Condition, Elevation, Emigration, and Destiny*, p. 65.
22. See Professor E. A. Ayandele's Introduction to the reprint of Bowen's work. T. J. Bowen, *Adventures and Missionary Labours in Several Countries in the Interior of Africa from 1849–1856*, 2d ed. (London: Frank Cass, 1968), p. vii.

Chapter 5

1. Edmund Ashworth to W. Seymour, Undersecretary of State, 30 May 1859, and Henry Christy to Lord John Russell, 29 July 1859, F. O. 2/30/1859, Public Records Office, London (hereafter cited as PRO).
2. Coppinger to Gurley, June 1859, and G. Ralston to Gurley, 24 June 1859, ACS Papers, 155, 156.
3. Foreign Office to Consul Lodder, 11 June 1859; Foreign Office to Ashworth, 11 June, and Christy, 22 August 1859, F.O. 2/30/1859, PRO.
4. Henry Venn to Henry Townsend, 23 October 1859, Church Missionary Society Papers, CA2/L2 (hereafter cited as CMS Papers).
5. See Alexander Crummell, *The Future of Africa* (New York: Charles Scribner, 1862).
6. Robert Campbell, *A Pilgrimage to My Motherland: An Account of a Journey Among the Egbas and Yorubas of Central Africa, in 1859–60* (New York: T. Hamilton, 1861), p. 11.
7. *Weekly Anglo-African*, 7 October 1859.
8. Robert Campbell, *A Few Facts Relating to Lagos, Abeokuta, and Other Sections of Central Africa* (Philadelphia: King and Baird, 1860), p. 5.
9. Stephen A. Benson to R. R. Gurley, 1 August 1859 and 13 July 1860 ACS Papers, 9, 10.
10. *Weekly Anglo-African*, 1 October 1859.
11. J. J. Roberts to Gurley, 28 July 1859, ACS Papers, 9.
12. *Weekly Anglo-African*, 1 October 1859.
13. Delany, *Niger Valley Exploring Party*, pp. 19, 23.
14. Ibid., pp. 24, 25–26.
15. Campbell, *Facts Relating to Lagos, Abeokuta*, p. 4.
16. Delany, *Niger Valley Exploring Party*, p. 29.
17. *Declaration of the Abeokuta Road-Improving Society*, 30 September 1859, in CMS Papers, CA2/O32.
18. Russell to Consul Brand, 17 March; Brand to Russell, 30 December 1860, Parliamentary Papers, 1860 LXX, Institute for Historical Research, London (hereafter cited as PP).

134 MARTIN R. DELANY AND THE AFRICAN DREAM

19. Notice of the Abeokuta Lyceum, Enclosed in CMS Papers, CA2/032.
20. Samuel Crowther, Jr., to Venn, 5 February 1860, CMS Papers, CA2/M4.
21. Delany, *Niger Valley Exploring Party*, p. 35.
22. J. F. Ade Ajayi, *Christian Missions in Nigeria 1841–1891, the Making of a New Elite* (London: Longmans, Green and Co., 1965), p. 97.
23. R. H. Stone to James B. Taylor, 2 February 1860, Southern Baptist Convention Missionary Society Papers 53/OY/39 (hereafter cited as SBCMS Papers).
24. T. A. Reid to A. M. Poindexter, 2 December 1859; Reid to Taylor, 25 January 1860, Ibid.
25. *Glasgow Daily Herald*, 9 October 1860; *Glasgow Examiner*, 13 October 1860.
26. Delany, *Niger Valley Exploring Party*, pp. 32–33.
27. Ibid., p. 40; Campbell, *Pilgrimage to Motherland*, p. 64.
28. J. F. Ade Ajayi and Robert Smith, *Yoruba Warfare in the Nineteenth Century* (New York: Cambridge University Press, 1964), p. 76–80.
29. Campbell, *Pilgrimage to Motherland*, pp. 115–23; Delany, *Niger Valley Exploring Party*, p. 37.
30. Delany, *Niger Valley Exploring Party*, p. 36.
31. T. B. Macaulay to Venn, 9 April 1860, CMS Papers, CA2/M4; Brand to Russell, 10 April 1860, 1861.
32. Dr. Thomas Hodgkin to Dr. N. Shaw, 6 June 1860; Delany to Shaw, 9, 15 June 1860, Royal Geographical Society Papers, Royal Geographical Society Archives, London (hereafter cited as RGSA Papers).
33. African Aid Society, 18 July 1860, RGSA Papers.
34. Howard Temperley, *British Anti-Slavery, 1833–1870* (Columbia: University of South Carolina Press, 1972), p. 40; Frank J. Klingberg, *The Anti-Slavery Movement in England* (New York: Archon Books, 1968), pp. 254–57.
35. Peter Henry Brougham, *Address of Lord Brougham, President, in Opening the Congress of the National Association for Promoting Social Science* (Glasgow: Richard Griffin and Company, 1860), p. 35.
36. The letters of Longstreet that revealed his emotional outbursts in the Delany affair are recorded in Rollin, *Life and Services of Delany*, pp. 104–15.
37. Ibid., p. 128; Benjamin Brawley, *Early Negro American Writers* (Chapel Hill: University of North Carolina Press, 1935), p. 218.
38. *Report of the Proceedings of the Fourth Session of the International Statistical Congress* (London: Her Majesty's Stationary Office, 1861), p. 285.
39. *Glasgow Daily Herald*, 9 October 1860.
40. *Glasgow Examiner*, 27 October 1860.
41. *North British Daily Mail*, 10 October 1860; *Morning Journal*, 11 October 1860; *Glasgow Examiner*, 27 October, 1860.
42. *Weekly Anglo-African*, 30 June, 7 October 1860.
43. *Glasgow Daily Herald*, 9 October 1860.
44. *Douglass' Monthly*, August 1862.

Chapter 6

1. William Coppinger to Gurley, 25 November 1860, ACS Papers, 161; Campbell to Russell, 23 July 1861, F.O. 84/1160/1861.

2. Robert Forster to Russell, 3 August 1861; Campbell to Russell, 23 July 1861, F.O. 84/1160/1861; Foreign Office to Campbell and Forster, 10 August 1861, and Foreign Office to Churchill, 10 August 1861, F.O. 84/1158/1861.
3. *Chatham Weekly Planet*, 26 January 1861; *Weekly Anglo-African*, 2 November, 7 December 1861 and 1 February 1862.
4. *Chatham Weekly Planet*, 26 January 1861.
5. Ibid.
6. Ibid., 21 February 1861.
7. *Weekly Anglo-African*, 10 August 1861.
8. Hubert Herring, *A History of Latin America from the Beginnings to the Present* (New York: Alfred A. Knopf, 1968), p. 430.
9. *Weekly Anglo-African*, 10 August 1861.
10. Coppinger to Gurley, 20 December 1860, ACS Papers, 165; and John Brown, Jr., to Redpath, 25 March 1861, James Redpath Papers (hereafter cited as JRP).
11. W. Honeybun to James Redpath, August n.d.; and Redpath to M. Plesance, 24 August 1861, JRP.
12. *Weekly Anglo-African*, 28 September 1861.
13. Ibid., 26 October 1861.
14. All of these complaints were recorded in the *Weekly Anglo-African* from 22 February to 5 April 1862.
15. Ibid., 25 January 1862.
16. Ibid., 2 November 1861.
17. Herring, *A History of Latin America*, pp. 427-29.
18. *Weekly Anglo-African*, 1 February 1862.
19. W. M. Brewer, "Henry Highland Garnet," *Journal of Negro History* 13 (1928): 48.
20. *Weekly Anglo-African*, 30 November 1861.
21. Ibid., 4, 25 January 1862.
22. Ibid., 1 February 1862.
23. T. Bourne to Gurley, 7 February 1859, ACS Papers; Howard Brotz, ed., *Negro Social and Political Thought* (New York: Basic Books, 1966), pp. 191-93.
24. Brotz, *Negro Social and Political Thought*, p. 266.
25. *Weekly Anglo-African*, 27 April 1861.
26. Ibid., 19 October, 9, 16 November 1861, 4 January 1862.
27. Ibid., 16, 30 November 1861.
28. Ibid., 4 January 1862.
29. Ibid., 16 November 1861.
30. Data for emigrants going from Canada to Yorubaland were found in correspondence of the African Aid Society, F.O. 84/1159/1861.
31. August Meier and Elliott M. Rudwick, *From Plantation to Ghetto* (New York: Hill and Wang, 1969), p. 142.
32. *Weekly Anglo-African*, 9 November 1861.
33. Ibid., 4 January 1862.
34. Ibid.
35. Ibid., 18 January 1862.
36. Ibid., 25 January 1862.
37. Ibid., 1 February 1862.
38. *Iwe Irohin*, 25 March, 5 April 1861.
39. Townsend to Venn, 6 February 1860, CMS Papers, CA2/085; Venn to David Hinderer, 19 January 1861, Ibid., CA2/L3; Venn to C. A. Gollmer, 23 March

1861, Ibid., CA3/L3; Saburi O. Biobaku, *The Egba and their Neighbours 1842–1872* (Oxford: Clarendon Press, 1957), pp. 71–72.
40. Townsend to Venn, 6 February 1860, CMS Papers, CA2/085.
41. Ibid.
42. Venn to the Lord Bishop of Oxford, 12 March 1859. This letter was printed in the *Cotton Supply Reporter*, 1 June 1859.
43. William King to David Livingstone, 12 September 1860; Livingstone to King, 15 February 1861, King Papers.
44. *Iwe Irohin*, 5 April 1861.
45. Rev. S. A. Crowther to F. Fitzgerald and Venn, 6 May 1861, CMS Papers, CA3/04(a).
46. A copy of the treaty was placed at the back of Campbell's book, *Pilgrimage to Motherland*, pp. 143–45.
47. Samuel Crowther, Jr., to Churchill, 18 April 1861, Enclosure 2 in No. 8, PP, 1861 LXI.
48. Ibid.
49. Ibid., Enclosure 3 in No. 8.
50. Rev. Crowther to Churchill, 5 January 1861, CMS Papers, CA3/04(a).
51. Consul Foote to Lord John Russell, 9 March 1861, No. 6, PP, 1861 LXI; Foreign Office to African Aid Society, 15 April 1861, F.O. 84/1158/1861.
52. Foote to Wylde, 6 April 1861, F.O. 84/1141/1816.
53. Foote to Russell, 9 March 1861, No. 6, PP, 1861 LXI.
54. Ibid., 5 October 1861.
55. *Douglass' Monthly*, August 1862.
56. Foreign Office to Manchester Chamber of Commerce, 19 January 1861. Printed in the *Cotton Supply Reporter*, 1 February 1861.
57. *Cotton Supply Reporter*, 15 January 1861.
58. Lord Wodehouse to Russell, 12 February, 30 March 1861, F.O. 84/1159; Wodehouse to Russell, 22 July 1861, F.O. 84/1160/1861.
59. Churchill to Foreign Office, 23 March 1861, F.O. 84/1159/1861.
60. Freeman to the Alake and Chiefs of Abeokuta, 14 June 1862, Enclosure 4 in No. 23, Russell to Freeman, 23 August 1862, Enclosure No. 25, PP, 1863 LXXI.
61. Freeman to Russell, 8 August 1862, No. 26, ibid. Bowen, *Adventures and Missionary Labours*, pp. xxviii–xxix; Ajayi, *Christian Missions in Nigeria*, pp. 189–91.
63. T. King to Colonel Dawes, 1 February 1862, CMS Papers, CA2/m4.
64. *African Times*, 23 January, 23 November 1863.
65. *Douglass' Monthly*, August 1862.
66. Ibid., September 1862.

Chapter 7

1. *Douglass' Monthly*, May 1861.
2. Delany to Edwin M. Stanton, 15 December 1863, Colored Troops Division Files (CTD), National Archives; Rollin, *Life and Public Services of Delany*, pp. 147, 149–50.
3. Poster "To Colored Men," CTD Files.

4. Poster to "Black National Defenders," Ibid.
5. Rollin, *Life and Public Services of Delany*, p. 309.
6. Brewer, "Henry Highland Garnet," pp. 48–50.
7. Rollin, *Life and Public Services of Delany*, pp. 168–69.
8. Colonel C. W. Foster to Captain Henry Keteltas, 27 February 1865; Delany to Colonel C. W. Foster, n.d.; Foster to General Rufus Saxton and General E. D. Townsend to Department of the South, 27 February 1865, CTD Files.
9. Foster to Delany, 27 March 1865. Ibid.
10. General R. K. Scott to Colonel H. W. Smith, 11 June 1866, Ibid.
11. *Charleston Courier*, 10 May 1865.
12. Ibid., 13 May 1865.
13. Ibid.
14. Lieutenant E. M. Stoeber to Major S. M. Taylor, 24 July 1865, CTD Files.
15. Ibid.
16. Lieutenant Alexander Whyte, Jr., to Major General G. A. Gillmore, 10 August 1865, Ibid.
17. Herbert Aptheker, "South Carolina Negro Conventions, 1865," *Journal of Negro History* 31 (1946): 95–97.
18. Ibid., p. 248.
19. General Ulysses S. Grant to Headquarters of Second Military District, Charleston, 4 December 1867, and General Thomas M. Vincent to Major M. R. Delany, 8 February 1868, Freedmen's Bureau Records (hereafter cited as FBR).
20. General R. K. Scott to General O. O. Howard, 22 July 1868, Ibid.
21. Martin R. Delany, *A Series of Four Tracts on Ntaional Polity, To the Students of Wilberforce University, Being Adapted to the Capacity of the Newly Enfranchised Citizens, First Series* (Charleston, S.C.: Republican Book and Job Office, 1870), pp. 5–8. These tracts were published first as articles in successive issues of the *New Era* from 27 January to 10 March 1870.
22. Delany, *Four Tracts on National Polity*, p. 9.
23. Ibid., p. 11.
24. Ibid., p. 13.
25. Philip S. Foner, *The Life and Writings of Frederick Douglass* (New York: International Publishers, 1955): 2:276–77.
26. Ibid., p. 278.
27. Ibid., p. 279.
28. W. E. B. DuBois, *Black Reconstruction . . . in America, 1860–1880* (New York: Meridian Books Edition, 1868), pp. 402–3.
29. Captain J. W. Loyd to Governor R. K. Scott, 7 November 1871, Box 18, Folder 15, Scott Papers.
30. Delany to Coppinger, 18 August 1880, ACS Papers, 240.
31. Delany to Scott, 25 March 1871, Box 15, Folder 23, Scott Papers; Delany to Coppinger, 18 August 1880, ACS Papers, 240.
32. *Beaufort Republican*, 25 April 1872.
33. Ibid., 3 October 1872.
34. Rev. Richard H. Cain to Governor Franklin J. Moses, Jr., 8 May 1873, Box 4, Folder 3, Moses Papers.
35. *Missionary Record*, 5 July 1873.
36. *News and Courier*, 12 September 1874.
37. Ibid., 24 October 1874.

38. *New York World*, 6 March 1875.
39. *News and Courier*, 9 March 1875.
40. Ibid., 3, 4 January 1876.
41. Ibid., 30 June 1875.
42. Victor Ullman, *Martin R. Delany, The Beginnings of Black Nationalism* (Boston: Beacon Press, 1971), p. 469.
43. George E. Johnston and Aaron Logan to Governor D. H. Chamberlain, 16 August 1876, Box 14, Folder 4, Chamberlain Papers.
44. *News and Courier*, 7 December 1875, 13, 26–27 January, 15–16 May, 20, 22 June 1876.
45. Ibid., 16 October 1876.
46. Ibid., 18 October 1876.
47. J. G. Randall and David Donald, *The Civil War and Reconstruction* (Boston: D. C. Heath and Company, 1961), pp. 689–90.

Chapter 8

1. Rollin, *Life and Public Services of Delany*, p. 314.
2. Ibid., p. 315.
3. Ibid., p. 317.
4. Africanists refer to this view of African development as the Hamitic hypothesis. In the last decade it has been questioned seriously by some scholars, who felt that it was not an objective appraisal of African history. For a general discussion of the Hamitic hypothesis see Edith R. Sanders, "The Hamitic Hypothesis; Its Origin and Functions in Time Perspective," *Journal of African History* 10 (1969): 521–32.
5. Rollin, *Life and Public Services of Delany*, p. 318.
6. Ibid., p. 323.
7. Ibid., p. 326.
8. Martin R. Delany, *The Principia of Ethnology: The Origin of Races and Color, with an Archaeological Compendium of Ethiopian and Egyptian Civilization, from Years of Careful Examination and Enquiry* (Philadelphia: Harper and Row, 1879), p. 9.
9. Ibid., p. 15.
10. August Meier, *Negro Thought in America, 1880–1915* (Ann Arbor: University of Michigan Press, 1963), p. 60.
11. H. N. Bouey to Coppinger, Bouey to Henry M. Turner, 23 May 1877, ACS Papers, 227.
12. *News and Courier*, 16 April 1878.
13. *African Repository* 53 (October 1877): 115–16.
14. B. F. Porter to President James S. Payne, 6 November 1877, Ibid. 54 (July 1878): 75.
15. Ibid., p. 77.
16. Ibid., pp. 77–78, and 55 (January 1879): 19, (April 1879): 37.
17. Ibid., 54 (July 1878): p. 78.
18. Delany to Latrobe, 8 July 1878, ACS Papers, 232.
19. Ibid.

20. Delany to Eli K. Price, 17 July 1878; Price to Coppinger, 7 August 1878, Ibid.
21. Latrobe to Coppinger, 16 July 1878, Ibid.
22. John Orcutt to Coppinger, 27 July 1878, Ibid.
23. Isaac S. Smith to Coppinger, 29 July 1878, Ibid.
24. *African Repository* 54 (July 1878): 78.
25. Ibid., p. 85.
26. Ibid. 55 (April 1879): 37.
27. E. Willis to Coppinger, 12 January 1880, ACS Papers, 238; Delany to Coppinger, 18 August 1880, Ibid., 240.
28. Willis to Coppinger, 9 March 1880, Ibid., 238.
29. Delany to Coppinger, 18 August 1880, Ibid., 240.
30. Abraham Burke to Coppinger, 19 June 1879, Ibid., 235.
31. *Proceedings of the Twentieth Quadrennial Session of the General Conference of the African Methodist Episcopal Church* (Wilmington, N.C., 4 May 1896), pp. 83–84.
32. Bishop Turner's place in the history of back-to-Africa movements is adequately dealt with in Edwin S. Redkey, *Black Exodus, Black Nationalist and Back-to-Africa Movements, 1890–1910* (New Haven: Yale University Press, 1969).
33. *African Repository* 51 (January 1875): 39; 52 (July 1876): 83.
34. Ibid., pp. 84–85.
35. Ibid. 55 (October 1879): 104.
36. Ibid. 56 (October 1880): 109.
37. Ibid. 57 (February 1881): 20.
38. George B. Tindall, *South Carolina Negroes 1877–1900* (Baton Rouge: Louisiana State University Press, 1966), p. 167; *African Repository* 66 (January 1890): 28–29.
39. Delany to Coppinger, 18 August, 6 September 1880, ACS Papers, 240.
40. Delany to Coppinger, 7 February, 11, 13, 15 March 1882, Ibid., 246.
41. Brawley, *Negro Writers*, p. 218; *Cleveland Gazette*, 21 February 1885.
42. *Xenia Daily Gazette*, 24 January 1885.
43. Ibid., 7 January 1885.
44. *News and Courier*, 8 February 1885.

Epilogue

1. Daniel A. Payne, *Recollections of Seventy Years* (Nashville, Tenn.: A.M.E. Sunday School Union, 1888), p. 160.
2. See George Shepperson, "Notes on Negro American Influences on the Emergence of African Nationalism," *Journal of African History* 1 (1960): 300.
3. Adelaide Cromwell Hill and Martin Kilson, eds., *Apropos of Africa* (Garden City, N.Y.: Doubleday and Company, 1971), pp. 26–36; Raymond F. Betts, ed., *The Ideology of Blackness* (Lexington, Mass.: D.C. Heath and Company, 1971), pp. 22–24; Brotz, *Negro Social and Political Thought*, pp. 37–111.
4. Howard H. Bell, *Search for a Place, Black Separatism and Africa, 1860* (Ann Arbor: University of Michigan Press, 1971), pp. 27–148.

Selected Bibliography

Manuscripts in England

Papers of the Church Missionary Society's Yoruba and Niger Missions. CMS Archives, London. These papers include the letters of Henry Venn and Henry Townsend; many of them contain their opinions of Delany's activities in Yorubaland.

Papers of the Methodist Missionary Society, Gold Coast Files, 1859–1861. MMS Archives, London. Letters of Rev. Thomas Champness in these papers shed some light on the controversy in Abeokuta over Delany's treaty.

Papers of the Royal Geographical Society. RGS Archives, London. These papers contain correspondence between Delany and members of the society.

Documents at the Public Record Office, London. F.O. 2/28/1859 Africa, Consular Records; F.O. 2/30/2859 Africa, Consular Records; F.O. 2/42/1862 Africa, Consular Records; F.O. 84/1141/1861 Slave Trade Correspondence; F.O. 84/1158/1861 Slave Trade Correspondence; F.O. 84/1159/1861 Slave Trade Correspondence; F.O. 84/1160/1861 Slave Trade Correspondence. These volumes have many letters by Secretary of State Lord John Russell and consuls at Lagos, which include data on Delany, Robert Campbell, and the African Aid Society.

Parliamentary Papers. Institute for Historical Research, London. 1860 LXX Slave Trade Correspondence, Class B; 1861 LXI Slave Trade Correspondence, Class B; 1863 LXXI Slave Trade Correspondence, Class B. These volumes also include letters that give some information on Delany's activities in Yorubaland.

Manuscripts in Nigeria

Papers of the Church Missionary Society, Yoruba Mission. Africana Collection, University of Ibadan. Among these papers are the letters of Bishop Samuel Crowther and his son Samuel Crowther, Jr., who were supporters of Delany.

Papers of the Southern Baptist Convention Missionary Society, Yoruba Mission. Africana Collection, University of Ibadan. Various letters of R. H. Stone, James B. Taylor, T. A. Reid, and A. M. Poindexter revealed their sympathy for Delany's emigration scheme.

Manuscripts in Canada and the United States

American Colonization Society Papers. Manuscript Collection, Library of Congress. These papers contain material about Delany's association with the Liberia Exodus Movement and his efforts to return to Liberia prior to his death.

Colored Troops Division Files, National Archives, Washington, D.C.

Freedmen's Bureau Records, National Archives, Washington, D.C. These sources at the National Archives have considerable information on Delany's brief career in the United States Army along with some of his political speeches in South Carolina.

Papers of Governors Daniel H. Chamberlain, R. K. Scott, and Franklin J. Moses, Columbia, South Carolina. Many letters in these collections contain information on Delany's political activities in South Carolina.

Medical School Records, Harvard Medical School. Harvard University, Boston.

Minutes and Records of the Harvard Medical School Faculty, Widener Library. Harvard University, Boston. Correspondence in these sources explain why Delany did not graduate from Harvard's Medical School.

Rev. William King Papers. Chatham Public Library, Chatham, Ontario. King was interested in the Niger Valley Exploring Party because Delany hoped to take blacks from the community he founded (Buxton) to West Africa.

Published Works of Martin R. Delany

Delany, Martin R. *Chief Commissioner, Africa, Official Report of the Niger Valley Exploring Party.* New York: T. Hamilton, 1861.

———. *The Condition, Elevation, Emigration, and Destiny of the Colored People of the United States.* Philadelphia: Published by the author, 1852.

———. *The Origin and Objectives of Ancient Freemasonry; Its Introduction into the United States, and Legitimacy Among Colored Men.* Pittsburgh: W. S. Haven, 1853.

———. *The Principia of Ethnology: The Origin of Races and Color, with an Archaeological Compendium of Ethiopian and Egyptian Civilization, from Years of Careful Examination and Enquiry.* Philadelphia: Harper and Bros., 1879.

———. *A Series of Four Tracts on National Polity, To the Students of Wilberforce University, Being Adapted to the Capacity of the Newly Enfranchised Citizens, First Series.* Charleston, S.C.: Republican Book and Job Office, 1870.

Other Published Works

Books and Pamphlets

Ajayi, J. F. Ade. *Christian Missions in Nigeria 1841–1891, the Making of a New Elite.* London: Longmans, Green and Co., 1965.

Ajayi, J. F. Ade, and Smith, Robert. *Yoruba Warfare in the Nineteenth Century.* New York: Cambridge University Press, 1964.

Amelio, Louis P. *Brave Black Regiment.* Boston: Boston Book Company, 1894.

Anderson, Osborne Perry. *A Voice from Harper's Ferry.* Boston: Printed by the author, 1861.

Bell, Howard H. *Search for a Place, Black Separatism and Africa, 1860.* Ann Arbor: University of Michigan Press, 1971.

Betts, Raymond F., ed. *The Ideology of Blackness.* Lexington, Mass.: D. C. Heath and Company, 1971.

Biobaku, Saburi O. *The Egba and their Neighbours, 1842–1872.* Oxford: Clarendon Press, 1957.

Boan, Josephus R. *Daniel Alexander Payne—Christian Educator.* Philadelphia: A.M.E. Book Concern, 1935.

Bowen, T. J. *Adventures and Missionary Labours in Several Counties in the Interior of Africa from 1849–1856.* 2d ed. London: Frank Cass, 1968.

Brawley, Benjamin. *A Social History of the American Negro.* New York: The Macmillan Co., 1921.

———. *Early Negro American Writers.* Chapel Hill: University of North Carolina Press, 1935.

Brotz, Howard, ed. *Negro Social and Political Thought.* New York: Basic Books, 1966.

Brougham, Peter Henry. *Address of Lord Brougham, President, in Opening the Congress of the National Association for Promoting Social Science.* Glasgow: Richard Griffin and Company, 1860.

Butler, Jeffrey, ed. *Boston University Papers on Africa.* Boston: Boston University Press, 1966.

Campbell, Robert. *A Few Facts Relating to Lagos, Abeokuta, and Other Sections of Central Africa.* Philadelphia: King and Baird, 1860.

———. *A Pilgrimage to My Motherland: An Account of a Journey Among the Egbas and Yorubas of Central Africa, in 1859–60.* New York: T. Hamilton, 1861.

Clendenen, Clarence C., and Duignan, Peter. *Americans in Black Africa.* Stanford, Ca.: Hoover Institution of War, Revolution, and Peace, 1964.

Cromwell, John Wesley. *The Early Negro Convention Movement.* Washington, D.C.: The American Negro Academy, 1904.

Crummell, Alexander. *The Future of Africa.* New York: Charles Scribner, 1862.

Cruse, Harold. *The Crisis of the Negro Intellectual.* New York: William Morrow and Company, 1967.

DuBois, W. E. B. *Black Reconstruction, an Essay Toward a History of the Part which Black Folk Played in the Attempt to Reconstruct Democracy in America, 1860–1880.* New York: Meridan Books Edition, 1968.

———. *John Brown.* New York: International Publishers, 1962.

———. *The Philadelphia Negro: A Social Study.* 2d ed. New York: Benjamin Blum, 1967.

Detweiler, Frederick G. *The Negro Press in the United States.* Chicago: University of Chicago Press, 1922.

Draper, Theodore. *The Rediscovery of Black Nationalism.* New York: Viking Press, 1964.

Foner, Philip S. *Frederick Douglass.* New York: The Citadel Press, 1969.

———. *The Life and Writings of Frederick Douglass*. 4 vols. New York: International Publishers, 1955.
Gysin, Brian. *To Master—A Long Goodnight*. New York: Creative Age Press, 1946.
Herring, Hubert. *A History of Latin America from the Beginnings to the Present*. New York: Alfred A. Knopf, 1968.
Hill, Adelaide Cromwell, and Kilson, Martin, eds. *Apropos of Africa*. Garden City, N.Y.: Doubleday and Company, 1971.
Klingberg, Frank J. *The Anti-Slavery Movement in England*. New York: Archon Books, 1968.
Kopytoff, Jean Herskovits. *A Preface to Modern Nigeria: The "Sierra Leonians" in Yoruba, 1830–1890*. Madison: University of Wisconsin Press, 1965.
Logan, Rayford. *The Negro in the United States*. Princeton, N.J.: Van Nostrand, 1957.
Loggins, Vernon. *The Negro Author*. New York: Columbia University Press, 1931.
Lucas, J. Olumide. *The Religion of the Yorubas*. Lagos: C.M.S. Bookshop, 1948.
Lynch, Hollis R. *Edward Wilmot Blyden, Pan-Negro Patriot*. London: Oxford University Press, 1967.
Meier, August. *Negro Thought in America, 1880–1915*. Ann Arbor: University of Michigan Press, 1963.
———, and Rudwick, Elliott M. *From Plantation to Ghetto*. New York: Hill and Wang, 1969.
Miller, Floyd J., ed. *Blake or the Huts of America*. Boston: Beacon Press, 1970.
Minutes and Proceedings of the General Convention of the Colored Inhabitants of Canada. Amherstburg, Ontario, 16–17 June 1853.
Parrinder, G. *West African Religion*. London: Epworth Press, 1961.
Payne, Daniel A. *Recollections of Seventy Years*. Nashville, Tenn.: A.M.E. Sunday School Union, 1888.
Proceedings of the National Emigration Convention of Colored People: held at Cleveland, August, 1854. Pittsburgh: A. A. Anderson, 1854.
Proceedings of the Twentieth Quadrennial Session of the General Conference of the African Methodist Episcopal Church. Wilmington, N.C.: 4 May 1896.
Quarles, Benjamin. *Black Abolitionists*. New York: Oxford University Press, 1969.
———. *The Negro in the Civil War*. New York: Russell and Russell, 1968.
Randall, J. G., and Donald, David. *The Civil War and Reconstruction*. Boston: D. C. Heath and Company, 1961.
Redkey, Edwin S. *Black Exodus, Black Nationalist and Back-to-Africa Movements, 1890–1910*. New Haven: Yale University Press, 1969.
Report of the Proceedings of the Fourth Session of the International Statistical Congress. London: Her Majesty's Stationary Office, 1861.
Rollin, Frank A. *Life and Public Services of Martin R. Delany*. Boston: Lee and Sheppard, 1868.
Shadd, Mary Ann. *A Plea for Emigration; Or, Notes of Canada West, in its Moral, Social, and Political Aspect*. Detroit: George W. Pattison, 1852.
Staudenraus, P. J. *The African Colonization Movement, 1816–1865*. New York: Columbia University Press, 1961.

Stephen, Leslie, and Lee, Sidney, eds. *The Dictionary of National Biography.* London: Oxford University Press, 1963–1964.

Sterling, Dorothy. *The Making of an Afro-American: Martin R. Delany, 1812–1885.* Garden City, N.Y.: Doubleday and Company, 1971.

Temperley, Howard. *British Antislavery, 1833–1870.* Columbia: University of South Carolina Press, 1972.

Tindall, George B. *South Carolina Negroes 1877–1900.* Baton Rouge: Louisiana State University Press, 1966.

Turner, Edward Raymond. *The Negro in Pennsylvania 1639–1861.* Washington, D.C.: American Historical Association, 1912.

Ullman, Victor. *Martin R. Delany, the Beginnings of Black Nationalism.* Boston: Beacon Press, 1971.

Walker, F. D. *A Hundred Years in Nigeria. The Story of the Methodist Mission, 1842–1942.* London: Cargate Press, 1943.

Whitfield, James M. *America, and Other Poems.* Buffalo: James S. Leavitt, 1853.

Williams, G. W. *History of the Negro Race in America.* 2 vols. New York: G. P. Putnam's Sons, 1883.

Winks, Robin W. *Canada and the United States: The Civil War Years.* Baltimore: Johns Hopkins University Press, 1960.

Woodson, Carter G. *A Century of Negro Migration.* Washington, D.C.: The Association for the Study of Negro Life and History, 1918.

———. *The Mind of the Negro as Reflected in Letters During the Crisis, 1800–1860.* Washington, D.C.: Associated Publishers, 1926.

———. *Negro Makers of History.* Washington, D.C.: Associated Publishers, 1928.

———. *The Works of Francis Grimke.* Washington, D.C.: Associated Publishers, 1942.

Articles

Aptheker, Herbert. "South Carolina Negro Conventions, 1865," *Journal of Negro History* 31 (1946): 91–97.

Bell, Howard H. "The Negro Emigration Movement, 1849–1854: A Phase of Negro Nationalism," *Phylon* 20 (1959): 132–42.

———. "Expressions of Negro Militancy in the North, 1840–1860," *Journal of Negro History* 45 (January 1960): 11–20.

Brewer, W. M. "Henry Highland Garnet," *The Journal of Negro History* 13 (1928): 36–52.

DuBois, W. E. B. "Reconstruction, Seventy-Five Years After," *Phylon* 4 (1943): 205–12.

Holly, James T. "In Memoriam," *A.M.E. Church Review* 3 (October 1886): 117–25.

Kirk-Greene, A. H. M. "America in the Niger Valley: A Colonization Centenary," *Phylon* 23 (1962): 225–39.

Landon, Fred. "Social Conditions Among the Negroes in Upper Canada," *Ontario Historical Society Papers and Records* 22 (1925): 144–61.

———. "The Work of the American Missionary Association Among the Negro Refugees in Canada West, 1848–1864," *Ontario Historical Society Papers and Records* 21 (1923): 198–205.

Sanders, Edith R. "The Hamitic Hypothesis; Its Origin and Functions in Time Perspective," *Journal of African History* 10 (1969): 521-32.
Shepperson, George. "Notes on Negro American Influences on the Emergence of African Nationalism," *Journal of African History* 1 (1960): 299-312.
Sires, Ronald U. "Sir Henry Barkley and the Labor Problem in Jamaica, 1853-1856," *Journal of Negro History* 25 (1940): 216-35.

Newspapers and Journals

African Repository, Washington, D.C.
African Times, London.
Aliened American, Cleveland.
Anglo-African Magazine, New York.
Beaufort Republican, Beaufort.
Boston Journal, Boston.
Charleston Courier, Charleston.
Chatham Planet, Chatham.
Chatham Tri-Weekly Planet, Chatham.
Chatham Weekly Planet, Chatham.
Cincinnati Morning Herald, Cincinnati.
Cleveland Gazette, Cleveland.
Cleveland Morning Leader, Cleveland.
Cotton Supply Reporter, Manchester.
Daily Cleveland Herald, Cleveland.
Daily Morning Chronicle, Pittsburgh.
Daily Morning Post, Pittsburgh.
Douglass' Monthly, Rochester, N.Y.
Emancipator, Boston.
Frederick Douglass' Paper, Rochester, N.Y.
Glasgow Examiner, Glasgow.
Glasgow Daily Herald, Glasgow.
Glasgow Merchantile Advertiser, Glasgow.
Glasgow Morning Journal, Glasgow.
Iwe Irohin, Abeokuta.
Liberator, Boston.
Liberia Herald, Monrovia.
Missionary Record, Charleston.
Morning Journal, Glasgow.
New Era, Washington, D.C.
New York World, New York.
News and Courier, Charleston.
North British Daily Mail, Glasgow.
North Star, Rochester, N.Y.
Palladium of Liberty.
Pennsylvania Freeman, Philadelphia.
Port Royal Commercial, Port Royal.
Provincial Freeman, Chatham.
Voice of the Fugitive, Windsor.
Weekly Anglo-African, New York.
Xenia Daily Gazette, Xenia.

Index

Abegga, 49
Abeokuta (Western Nigeria), 40, 42-43, 47, 50-51, 73, 77
Abeokuta Lyceum, 48
Abeokuta Road-Improving Society, 47
Abstinence Society, 4
Accra, Ghana, 42
Adelu (Oyo king), 51-52
Africa: Afro-American rejection of, 115, 120
  civilizations in, 105
  emigration to, 17, 27
  Europeans in, 103
  Horn of, 37
  nationalism in, 120
  racial myths about, 102
African Aid Society, 52, 54, 56, 58-59, 62, 75, 79-80
African Christian Civilization Committee, 53
African Methodist Episcopal churches, 32
African Times, 80
Afro-American conventions, 8, 17, 23, 28, 90, 115
Afro-Americans: and annexation of Lagos, 69
  and pan-Africanism, 1
  economic conditions of, 9-10, 25
  emigration sentiments of, 24
  in the American Revolution, 82
  in the Union Army, 88
  leadership of, 7
  limited freedom of, 15
  political awareness of, 9
Afro-American emigration: to Canada, 17
  to Haiti, 65
  to Jamaica, 32
Afro-American press, 5
Afro-American Repository, 33
Alake (Egba ruler), 48, 74-75, 79, 81
Aliened American, 26, 28
Allegheny City, Pennsylvania, 12, 15
Allegheny County, Pennsylvania, 6
American and Foreign Bible Society, 108
American Baptist Publication Society, 108
American Colonization Society, 2, 14, 17, 23, 36, 38-39, 67, 106, 108-9, 111-13, 115, 117
American Free Baptist Mission, 65
American Geographical and Statistical Society, 58
American Revolution, 82
American Union Ethiopian Association, 114
Americo-Liberians, 45
Amherstburg Emigration Convention, 18
Andrew, John A., 82
Anglo-African (Lagos), 59
Anglo-Africans, 21
Annexation of Lagos, 40
Arabs, 103
Aray, Amos, 35-36
Are (ruler of Ijaye), 51-52

148 INDEX

Ashanti, 51
Ashworth, Edmund, 41
Association for the Promotion of the Interest of the Colored People of Canada and the United States, 34
Austin, William E., 6
Awaye (Western Nigeria), 52
Azor, 111-14, 116

Bacon, Leonard, 115
Bancroft, George, 116
Barclay, Alexander, 32
Battle of Honey Springs, 83
Beaufort Republican, 95
Bennett, John, 41
Benson, Stephen A., 42-44, 46
Berkshire Medical School, 12-13
Bibb, Henry, 16, 19
Bickersteth, Edward, 48
Black, Rev. A. W., 12
Black abolitionists, 2, 5, 7
Black codes, in Ohio, 9
  in Virginia, 3
Black diaspora, 22, 38, 58, 106
Black Mayflower, 108. See also *Azor*
Black nationalism, 1, 21-22
Black vigilantes, 4
Blair, Francis Preston, 31
Blyden, Edward Wilmot, 44-45, 66, 120
Bolorunpelu (Western Nigeria), 52
Boston, Massachusetts, 13
Bouey, H. N., 106, 116
Bourne, Theodore, 68
Bowen, Thomas Jefferson, 38, 67
Boyer, Jean Pierre, 65
Brazil, 22, 41, 46
British and Foreign Anti-Slavery Society, 68
British Foreign Office, 41
British Niger Expedition, 49
Bronwell, Anthony, 86
Brougham, Lord Henry Peter, 54-55
Brown, Bishop J. M., 114
Brown, Bishop Morris, 108
Brown, John, 33-34
Brown, John, Jr., 62-63
Brown, William Wells, 63, 72, 82
Bryant, William Cullen, 97
Buffalo, New York, 6

Burke, Abraham, 114
Burton, Richard Francis, 76
Buxton, Ontario, 34, 55, 63, 70

Cain, Rev. Richard H., 95-96, 110
Cainhoy, South Carolina, 101
Cambridge, Massachusetts, 14
Campbell, Benjamin (British consul), 52
Campbell, Bishop Jabez T., 115
Campbell, George John Douglas (eighth Duke of Argyll), 105
Campbell, Robert, 34-36, 41-43, 47-53, 57-58, 68, 109, 121
Campbell, S. J., 114
Cape Coast, Ghana, 42
Cape Palmas, Liberia, 42, 46
Cardozo, Francis L., 95
Careysburg, Liberia, 45
Carr, Rev. A. T., 114
Central America, 22, 27, 31
Chamberlain, Daniel H., 97, 99-100
Chambersburg, Pennsylvania, 3
Champness, Rev. Thomas, 79
Charleston, South Carolina, 88, 113
Charlestown, West Virginia, 2
Chase, Salmon P., 87-88
Chatham, Ontario, 23-24, 32, 35, 63, 65, 70, 84
Chicago, Illinois, 82
Childs, Professor Henry H., 13
Chillicothe, Ohio, 8
Christian Advocate, 45
Christy, Henry, 41
Church Missionary Society, 40-41, 49, 73, 79
Churchill, Lord Alfred, 53, 59, 75, 77-78
Cincinnati, Ohio, 10
Civil Rights movement, 2, 120
Civil War, 1, 82, 87, 90, 92
Clapperton, Hugh, 38
Clark, Jackson, 116
Cleveland, Ohio, 23, 26, 32
Colonialism, in Latin America, 22
Colonizationists: a definition of, 2
  and Liberia Exodus movement, 109-12
Colored Troops, 104th Regiment of, 86-87

Columbiana, Ohio, 10
Columbus, Ohio, 6, 8
Committee of Colored Voters, 33
Confiscation Act (1861), 72
Constitution (United States), 92
Cooper, Peter, 7
Coppinger, William, 36, 109-12, 114, 117
Crowther, Rev. Samuel, 43, 52, 74-75
Crowther, Samuel, Jr., 43, 47-48, 74-76
Crum, Graham and Co., 56
Crummell, Alexander, 42, 120
Cruse, Harold, 2
Cuba, 41, 46
Cuffe, Paul, 120

Dahomey, 51
Day, William Howard, 26, 28, 34-35
Delany, Alexander Dumas, 5, 84
Delany, Faustin Soulouque, 5, 84
Delany, Martin R.: as emigrationist: address to emigrationists, 26-27; ignored critics, 29; associated with Liberia Exodus movement, 109-11; attends Toronto convention, 17-18; called for national convention, 23-24; sought West Indian cooperation, 31-32; views on emigration, 16, 19, 22; views on Haitian emigration movement, 60-61, 64-65
  as journalist: co-editor of the *North Star*, 8; conflict with Frederick Douglass, 11-12; published the *Mystery*, 5-7
  as pan-Africanist: defended African history and culture, 102-4, 118, 120-21; drift toward pan-Africanism, 32; obsession with Africa, 1; pan-African views expressed, 37, 39, 60, 71, 106; tried to return to Africa, 116-17, 119
  back-to-Africa movement: alliance with African Civilization Society, 69-71; appreciation of African culture, 50-51; journey to Africa, 43-47; lecture tour in Britain, 52-57; opposition to Liberia, 2-3; refused to join John Brown, 33-34, 132n; return and lecture tour in United States, 58-60; travels in Yorubaland, 48-52; treaty with Egba authorities, 48-49; validity of Egba treaty challenged, 73-76; Yorubaland scheme, 39
  background and personal life: birth and childhood, 2-3; his children, 5, 84, 113; his death, 118; marriage, 5; moved family to Canada, 32; moved family to Wilberforce, 84
  black nationalist: called for black army 82-84; emphasized black nationalism, 14, 88-89, 91-93, 97; motivations for nationalism, 4; nationalistic ideas, 24-25, 27, 57; views on cultural awareness, 21
  military career: entered Union Army, 86; left the Army, 91; recruiter, 82; worked with Freedmen's Bureau, 87-88
  political activities: appointed judge, 98; difficulties with Republicans, 94-96; in Canada, 33; stated political rights of blacks, 92-93; supported Democrats, 100-101; tried for embezzling, 99
Delany, Rameses Placido, 5
Delany, St. Cyprian, 113
Delany, Toussaint L'Ouverture, 5
Delany Rifles (Charleston, South Carolina), 94
Democrats, 91, 98, 100
Denham, Dixon, 38
Detroit, Michigan, 80, 87
Docemo (king of Lagos), 47
Douglas, H. Ford, 33
Douglass, Frederick, 7-9, 11-12, 19-20, 23, 25, 33, 54, 57
  criticized Delany, 81, 93-94
  opposed African Civilization Society, 67-68
  opposed emigration movement, 28
  partner of Delany, 15
  views on black troops, 82, 85
Douglass, Robert, 34-36
Douglass' Monthly, 76
Dresden, Ontario, 35, 66
DuBois, W. E. B., 9, 27, 94
Duffin, J. W., 64

INDEX

Eaton, General John, 95
Edisto Island, South Carolina, 101
Egba people, 40, 42, 78
Egba United Board of Management, 80
Egyptians, 103-4, 106
Elgin settlement, 34, 73. *See also* Buxton
Emancipation Proclamation, 72, 85-86
Emigration Convention (Chatham, Ontario), 34
Emigrationism, 2, 4, 14, 39, 105, 109-10
 Afro-American rejection of, 27-28, 71
 Bishop Turner and, 115-16
 tenets of, 18, 24-25
Emigrationists: a definition of, 2
 opposition to Liberia, 23
Ethiopia, 22
Ethiopians, 106
Explorers, 40

Faustin I (Emperor of Haiti), 65
Fifteenth Amendment, 100
Fifty-Fourth Colored Regiment, 82
First Kansas Colored Regiment, 83
First Regiment of Rhode Island Heavy Artillery, 83
Fisher, J. T., 17
Flegler, Rev. S., 108, 114
Foote, John (British consul), 75-76
Foster, Colonel C. W., 86-87
Fourteenth Amendment, 91
Fourth Ward Democratic Club (Charleston, South Carolina), 110
Frazier, Rev. David, 116
Frederick Douglass' Paper, 26
Freedmen's Bureau, 89, 94-95
Freedmen's Savings Bank, 100
Freeman, M. H., 34
Freetown, Sierra Leone, 42, 108
Frelinghuysen, Frederick T., 117
Fugitive Slave Law, 16-17, 25, 27, 84
Fulani people, 40
Fuller, Rev. William J., 24

Gaines, John I., 28-29
Gambia River, 42
Garfield, James A., 117

Garnet, Rev. Henry Highland, 65, 68-69, 71, 117
Garrison, William Lloyd, 16, 63
Gazzam, Dr. Joseph P., 12
Geffrard, Fadbre, 61, 64-65
Gillmore, Major-General G. A., 89
Glasgow, Scotland, 55-57
Gleaves, Richard H., 97
Gliddon, George R., 105
Grant, President Ulysses S., 98
Green, Judge John T., 97
Gurley, R. R., 44

Haines, Rev. J. S., 114
Haiti, 21-22, 28, 31, 44, 58, 61
Haitian Bureau of Emigration (Boston, Massachusetts), 61
Haitian emigration movement, 60-64
Hamitic hypothesis, 138
Hampton, Wade, 100-101
Hampton's Red Shirts, 101
Harper, Liberia, 46
Harvard Medical School, 13
Harvard University, 13-14, 16
Hazeley, J. C., 107
Henson, Josiah, 34
Hilton Head, South Carolina, 87, 90
Hodgkin, Dr. Thomas, 41, 53, 68
Holly, Rev. James T., 2, 17, 24-25, 30-32, 60-61, 64, 71
Holmes, W. E., 112
Honest Government League, 97
Honeybun, William, 62
Howard, General O. O., 91

Ibadan, Western Nigeria, 49, 50-51
Ijaye, Western Nigeria, 49, 50, 51
Ijaye War (1860-1865), 51-52
Ilorin, Western Nigeria, 49-50
Independent Republicans, 95-97. *See also* Republicans
International Statistical Congress, 54, 80
Irons, Clement, 114, 116
Isehin, Western Nigeria, 52
Ishagga, Western Nigeria, 78
Iwe-Irohin, 73

Jamaica, 22, 58, 65
Jenkins, A. D., 28

John Wesley Methodist Church, John's Island, South Carolina, 99
Johnson, George W., 80
Johnson, J. D., 66
Johnson, Tom "Fiddler," 6
Jones, Isaiah, 64
Jones, John, 82
Jordon, Edward, 31

Kansas-Nebraska Act, 25
King, Rev. William, 34, 55, 73
Kingston Journal, 31
Kirk-Greene, A. H. M., 2
Kosoko (king of Lagos), 47

Lagos, Nigeria, 40–43, 78
Laing, Daniel, Jr., 13
Lambert, William, 25
Langston, John Mercer, 10, 82, 117
Latrobe, J. H. B., 109–11
Lee, General Robert E., 87
LeMoyne, Dr. F. Julius, 12
Liberia, 13–14, 21–23, 28, 34, 36, 40, 44, 107, 109, 116
Liberia Exodus Association. *See* Liberia Exodus movement
Liberia Exodus Joint Stock Steamship Co., 107, 109, 111–12
Liberia Exodus movement, 106–16
Liberia Herald, 45, 77
Lincoln, President Abraham, 84–85
Lincoln University, 84
Livingstone, David, 38, 56, 67, 73
London Anti-Slavery Society, 41
Longstreet, A. B., 54
Lynch, Professor Hollis R., 2

Macaulay, Rev. R. B., 52
MacLeod, J. Lyons, 53
Magna Carta, 92
Manchester Cotton Supply Association, 41, 52, 56, 58, 62, 76
Marseilles, Ohio, 10
Massachusetts Colonization Society, 13–14, 36
Massachusetts Fourth Colored Regiment, 83
McCarthy's Island, Gambia, 42
McDowell, Dr. Andrew N., 3
McKeller, Archie, 33

McKinley, W. J., 101
Mendi, 39, 43
Missionaries, 40, 73–74
Missouri Compromise, 25
Molson, Edmund B., 64
Monroe, Mary O., 64
Monroe, Rev. William C., 24, 64
Monrovia, Liberia, 42–43
Moses, Franklin J., Jr., 96
Mount Vaughan, Liberia, 46
Myers, Jonathan J., 34
Mystery, 5–7

National Association for Promoting Social Science, 55
National Club (London), 53
National Emigration Convention (1854), 23–24
Nell, William C., 24
New South, 90, 91
New York Colonization Society, 36, 111
New York World, 97
Newman, Rev. William R., 65–66
News and Courier, 95, 97, 98, 100, 101, 118
Niger River, 40, 49
Niger Valley Exploring Party, 35–36, 40, 41, 43–44, 48–49, 51–53, 57, 68
North American Emigration Convention (1851), 16
North American League of emigrants, 17
North American-West Indian Trading Association, 33
North Star, 10, 12

Ogun River, 43, 47
Ogunbonna (Balagun), 49, 75, 79
Okeho, Western Nigeria, 51
Old Oyo Empire, 51
Orcutt, John, 111
Oyo, Western Nigeria, 49, 51

Pan-Africanism, 1, 4, 14, 25, 32, 34, 115
Park, Mungo, 40
Parsons, C. L., 116
Payne, Bishop Daniel Alexander, 84, 119

INDEX

Payne, Rev. James S., 107
Pennsylvania Colonization Society, 36, 59, 109, 111
Perinchief, William R., 62
Philanthropic Society, 4
Pinney, J. B., 36, 111
Pittsburgh, Pennsylvania, 3, 6, 12, 15, 23, 26
Port Royal, South Carolina, 87
Porter, Rev. B. F., 106, 109-10
Price, Eli K., 111
Provincial Freeman, 23, 32, 33, 70
Pugh, F. J., 113
Purnell, J. W., 35-36

Quakers, 10
Queens College, Cambridge University, 42
Quinn, Bishop William Paul, 24

Rabba, Nigeria, 49
Rainey, Joseph H., 95
Ralston, Gerard, 41
Reconstruction, 91-94, 97, 115
Redpath, James, 31, 60, 62-63
Reid, R. A., 50
Remond, Charles Lenox, 5, 10, 82
Republicans, 91, 94-98
Richards, Cathrine A. (Delany's wife), 5
Roberts, J. J., 46
Rochester, New York, 7, 23, 80
Roy, Major J. P., 87
Royal Geographical Society, 53
Russell, Lord John, 48, 52, 59, 77-78

St. Helena Island, South Carolina, 88-90
St. Paul's River, 46
Scoble, John, 41
Scotland, 55
Scott, General R. K., 91, 95
Seabrook, E. B., 99
Seys, Rev. John, 43
Shadd, Ada T., 70
Shadd, Amelia, 70
Shadd, Isaac D., 35, 70
Shadd, Mary Ann, 16, 24, 32, 63
Shaki, Western Nigeria, 51
Shango (Yoruba deity), 2-3

Shepperson, Professor George, 2, 120
Shomoye (Basorun), 79-80
Shunk, Francis R., 6
Sickles, General Daniel E., 87, 91
Sierra Leone, 40, 48
Sierra Leonians, 34, 42-43, 81
Slavery, 4, 11, 25, 27, 51, 54, 102-3
Smith, Dr. J. B., 62
Smith, Dr. James McCune, 71-72, 85
Smith, Gerrit, 72
Smith, Isaac S., 111
Smyth, John H., 117
Snowden, Isaac H., 13
South America, 22, 115
Southampton, Virginia, 3
Southern Baptist Convention, 38
Southern Baptist Convention Missionary Society, 50
Stanton, Edwin M., 84
Star of Liberia, 45
Stearns, George L., 82
Stoeber, Lieutenant Edward M., 89
Stone, R. H., 50
Stowe, Harriet Beecher, 20-21
Sudanese people, 106
Sumner, Charles, 83

Taylor, James T., 17
Taylor, Thomas C., 78
Thomas, Rev. M., 53
Tilden, Samuel J., 100
Tinubu, Madam, 52
Tomlinson, R. H., 87-88, 95
Toronto, Ontario, 16, 17
Townsend, Henry, 73, 75, 79, 81
Tracy, Joseph, 36
Trinidad, 22
Tucker, David, 62
Turner, Nat, 3
Turner, Rev. Henry MacNeal, 108, 114-15, 120
Twenty-Ninth Regiment of Volunteers, 83

Venn, Rev. Henry, 41-42, 48, 52, 73
Vesey, Denmark, 88
Voice of the Fugitive, 16

Walker, William E., 72
War of 1812, 21

Watkins, William J., 28, 72
Webb, Charles Henry, 86
Webb, Rev. William, 26
Weekly Anglo-African, 61, 64, 66, 69, 71, 76
Wesleyan Missionary Society, 48
West Africa, 2, 45, 78
West Indians, 18, 31, 120
West Indies, 17, 22–23, 27, 33, 115
Western Ontario, 15, 34
Whitfield, James M., 25, 28–30, 32
Whyte, Lieutenant Alexander, Jr., 89
Wilberforce, Ohio, 84, 93
Wilberforce, William, 54
Wilberforce University, 84–85, 91
Willis, E., 113
Windsor, Ontario, 16, 63
Wodehouse, Lord, 77–78
Woodson, Rev. Louis, 3

Yates and Porterfield (shipping firm), 113
York, Pennsylvania, 8
Yoruba people, 3, 40, 50
Yorubaland, 34, 38, 40, 43–44, 47, 49, 53, 56, 58, 73, 109

Xenia Daily Gazette, 118